# HOW TO MAKE
# EFFECTIVE
# PRESENTATIONS

**SURVIVAL   SKILLS   FOR   SCHOLARS**

Managing Editor: Peter Labella

**Survival Skills for Scholars** provides you, the professor or advanced graduate student working in a college or university setting, with practical suggestions for making the most of your academic career. These brief, readable guides will help you with skills that you are required to master as a college professor but may have never been taught in graduate school. Using hands-on, jargon-free advice and examples, forms, lists, and suggestions for additional resources, experts on different aspects of academic life give invaluable tips on managing the day-to-day tasks of academia—effectively and efficiently.

*Volumes in This Series*

SURVIVAL SKILLS FOR SCHOLARS

# HOW TO MAKE EFFECTIVE PRESENTATIONS

## ELIZABETH P. TIERNEY

SAGE Publications

*International Educational and Professional Publisher*

Thousand Oaks   London   New Delhi

*For information address:*

 SAGE Publications, Inc.
2455 Teller Road
Thousand Oaks, California 91320
E-mail: order@sagepub.com

SAGE Publications, Ltd.
6 Bonhill Street
London EC2A 4PU
United Kingdom

SAGE Publications India Pvt. Ltd.
M-32 Market
Greater Kailash I
New Delhi 110 048 India

Printed in the United States of America

**Library of Congress Cataloging-in-Publication Data**

Tierney, Elizabeth P.
  How to make effective presentations / Elizabeth P. Tierney.
    p.   cm. — (Survival skills for scholars ; v. 16)
  Includes bibliographical references.
  ISBN 0-8039-5956-7 (c: alk. paper). — ISBN 0-8039-5957-5
(p: alk. paper)
  1. Business presentations. I. Title. II. Series.
HF5718.22.T53  1995
658.4'52—dc20                                      95-22885


96  97  98  99  10  9  8  7  6  5  4  3  2  1

Sage Production Editor:  Tricia K. Bennett
Sage Typesetter:  Janelle LeMaster

# Contents

# 1 | Introduction

*I often tell the story of the first time I gave a speech. I was so nervous that I kept my eyes closed through most of the monologue. I kept hoping that if I didn't look at them they would quietly go away. When I had finished, I opened my eyes and discovered that, unfortunately, my wish had been granted. There was only one person left in the audience. He was a bookish-looking fellow wearing a sour expression. Hoping to find some solace in this catastrophe, I asked him why he stayed. Still frowning, he replied, "I'm the next speaker."*
—Victor Kiam, American businessman

"I'll be OK."
"I'll be fine."
"It'll be over soon."

This might sound like the mutterings of a hospital patient who is being wheeled on a gurney to the operating room. Actually, they are the same reassurances that you might give yourself when you are introduced as the next speaker at a faculty meeting or conference, or when you enter a lecture theater, stare at the empty lectern, and realize that you are next—it's show time!

Then, the medical analogy falls apart. In the operating theater you lie on the table while skilled, competent professionals work on you. If you are speaking, however, *you* are doing the

1

work; you are not anesthetized or lying prone. You are wide awake and totally dependent on your own skills and competence, not on someone else's. Like the poor unfortunate on the gurney, you are worried. Being nervous is normal. Despite your experience with your students, standing before an audience is a scary experience. How scary? Well, the results of a survey conducted some years ago indicated that public speaking was perceived to be the second most frightening experience in a person's life. What was number one, you ask? Dying!

Whether it was a year ago or 20 years ago, recall the first class that you taught, and you'll know why making a presentation is so terrifying. There are good reasons: You are alone; you are unprotected; you are vulnerable to attack; and you are standing in front of other people who are sitting, who are looking at you, and who expect something from you—great things. No matter how much ego you have, you are convinced that you will make a fool of yourself, that you will risk looking bad in the eyes of your colleagues, friends, department chairs, or students. The individuals in that audience are in a position to make judgments about you, about what you know, or about your research methods, and they will. That prospect is unnerving.

While you are trying to reassure yourself like the hospital patient and failing to do so, you are also undermining what confidence you do have by asking yourself questions such as: Will I sound ponderous? Will I be invited back? Will I embarrass the department? Will I embarrass myself? Will I be asked a question I can't answer? Will I be promoted? Will I be humiliated? Such a barrage of questions produces anxiety, but remember that this is self-inflicted. You are doing it to yourself.

Giving a lecture, making a speech, delivering a paper, or being part of a panel does not have to be so disquieting or terrifying. The ideas and recommendations that you will read in this book are written to help you realize that although worrying is normal, it is possible to get past the fear. Effective presentation is not a gift from the gods to a select few. It is neither a mystery nor something you are taught at your mother's knee. Anyone can learn to speak well.

Presentation involves both a process and a product. Of course, having some innate talent does not hurt, but anyone with a basic understanding of some of the techniques involved in speaking will have a better understanding of how to hold an audience's attention, be it 5 around a table or 200 in an auditorium. Being aware of these techniques will help develop your strengths and diminish your weaknesses as a speaker and instructor. In addition, anyone who understands and accepts some underlying principles and techniques about presenting will be a speaker and lecturer who is more polished and confident. Anyone who accepts the importance of finding time to practice and to seek feedback will be more effective and self-aware. Anyone who develops the habit of asking some key preliminary questions will become a more successful speaker, one whose ideas are considered, whose recommendations are weighed, and who will earn the plaudits of the audience. Just as you have developed your teaching skills over time and are nervous but no longer terrified, you may seek opportunities to speak in public; you may even enjoy them. Teaching is a specific form of presentation. It demands some unique techniques that are not addressed here. Although many of the recommendations that are made here may be applied to instructional situations, this book is about presentation in general.

There are no startling revelations here, but, by the end of this chapter, you will have read the underlying principles of making successful presentations; subsequent chapters will address the techniques, the need for practice, and the key questions that you should ask before you speak, whatever the occasion. Although these principles are dealt with separately for analytical purposes, each one of them is an integral part of the whole act of talking to a group.

Specifically, each chapter focuses on an element of presentation, from a review of the communication process itself to the use of notes and the handling of visuals. However, read no further if your purpose is to learn manipulation or demagoguery. These pages are designed to help you become a more comfortable, believable, and effective speaker or lecturer, not an unethical or deceitful one. As you well know, taken to an extreme, effective speaking and image management can hide and even distort the truth.

Let's articulate some more of those prespeaking concerns, because getting them out in the open is healthy. For those of you newer to the profession, if you recognize yourself in some of the worries, perhaps you may not be so lonely knowing that you are not the only one feeling so miserable. Do you really think that you are the only one who has endured these self-doubts? You are not. Even senior faculty members and professional presenters—in fact, most people accustomed to speaking—feel queasy when they face an audience.

So, what are you really worried about? Do you think you will sound stupid? Do you worry that the audience knows more about the subject than you do? Do you worry that you are going to bore those people to death? Do you worry that you are going to forget what you had planned to say? Do you worry about going blank? Do you worry that the content will be confusing? Any one of these nagging questions has the potential to undermine your self-esteem, whether you are in front of an audience; at a dinner, a seminar, an interview, or a class; or at a board, department, or faculty meeting.

Behind the reassurances and those nagging questions lurks the real issue. You know in your heart that it is not your talk that is being judged. You are. Somehow, you think that your name, career, or reputation is at stake. With all that baggage, it is no wonder that surgery appears to be a more pleasant option than speaking. With a general or local anesthesia, you could sleep through the proceedings, or at least minimize the pain.

The degree of discomfort that speakers feel is revealed by their choice of words as they describe their feelings after they have given a talk: "I'm so relieved," or "I survived," and not "great" or "excited." They are settling for survival. But what you need to do to succeed is to turn the experience around and focus on the positive implications of giving a talk rather than on the negative ones.

This book is written not only to assist you in being more at ease with the process and with yourself but also because—as members of a business faculty might say—being an effective presenter gives you a competitive advantage. You will lecture better, run meetings better, talk at seminars better, and give conference speeches better. Humans have not been totally replaced by technology yet. We still communicate face-to-face, individually and in groups, and the more comfortable and effective you are as a speaker, the more opportunities you create for yourself, your department, or your college or university.

What is written in this book is based on my years of experience in education on the secondary and college levels coaching teachers and trainers, and, as an academic and consultant working with students, businessmen and -women, and university faculty and staff, as well as on my own experience as a speaker and lecturer. It is based on the mistakes I have made and on the lessons I have learned and continue to learn. For one, I will never forget that dark day many years ago when one of my own dreaded fears was realized. It was the day that I took one look at the lens of the camera in front of me, and, despite my planning and rehearsing, I remembered nothing. I blew the audition because my mind was a complete blank.

On the other hand, I will also never forget the delightful occasion when I decided to take a lengthy pause during a speech and could sense the power as the audience waited for my next words. I also have learned from attending meetings and conferences and from watching speakers. I suspect that I have learned the most, though, from watching the audience's response to the speakers to whom they are listening. I watch individuals nod off, stare out the window, glance at their watches, read newspapers, or mark papers. I have also watched the eager faces of students who are enthralled by what they are hearing. To repeat, these pages are written with the conviction that you can learn to give a more effective presentation, to be less nervous, and to have greater impact on those who are listening to you and thus, ultimately, on your growth, self-esteem, and reputation.

Let's begin by looking at the four principles that underlie all presentations. They are the following:

- You should be responsible to the audience.
- You should make conscious decisions about what you are presenting and not rely on your intuition alone.
- You should make decisions before, during, and after you speak.
- You should become aware of your own strengths and weaknesses as a presenter and practice using techniques that will enhance your talk.

Let's look at each one of these principles.

## Be Responsible to the Audience

Frequently, speakers are so self-absorbed that they forget about the people in front of them. They often behave like elementary school students who have been told to memorize a poem in order to recite it in class. Remember when recitation time came, and each student got up and recited the poem as quickly as possible, eyes glued to the floor, oblivious to books falling, cars honking, or doors slamming?

Have you ever heard or used the phrase, "Thanks for listening" at the end of a talk? Children do not say that; adults do. It is a revealing expression because it suggests that the audience made the effort on your behalf, when, in fact, you were working on theirs. If you, as a speaker, do all that you need to do in preparation and accept the responsibility that you have to be interesting, challenging, articulate, and entertaining, then you will not need to thank the audience for listening. They will listen, and they will thank *you* when it is over for the effort that *you* made for *them*. In other words, the responsibility you have to those people before you—be it students or colleagues—is to be clear, sensitive, and analytical. You need to determine what will work for that unique group listening to you. As you well know, time is a valuable resource. The audience at a conference or seminar is giving up its time; has chosen not to work on that research project, not to catch up on the latest journal, and not to meet with students; and may have traveled a great distance in order to hear what you have to say. The audience's motivation for attending may be quite different from that of a class but students make decisions as well about how to best use their time. Therefore, responsibility to the audience rests squarely on your shoulders.

## Make Conscious Decisions

You should make conscious decisions about what you are doing when you speak; do not rely on your intuition alone. In other words, do not rely solely on your gut instincts on that day to advise you what to do. To be effective, you should be thinking about every aspect of your talk—what you will wear, where and how you will stand, how to use your voice, and when to turn the overhead on or off.

For example, do you use transparencies just because lecturers use acetates? Do you wear the blue jacket because it is in the closet? Do you stand behind the table or lectern because there is one in the room? In other words, are you being reactive or proactive? You should be asking yourself: Is the blue jacket right for this particular occasion or is it too washed out or too strong? Are acetates necessary and, if so, what for and why? Should I stand behind the lectern or table? Should I have it removed? Will I look more remote or more involved? In other words, decide what you have to do to be effective on that unique occasion.

## Make Decisions
## Before, During, and After

This principle involves decision making as well. You should be prepared to make decisions before, during, and after you speak. No, not just about the color of the jacket, the number of acetates, or the use of the lectern. Many of the decisions are interdependent.

For example, if you know that you have 30 minutes to speak, then, as you would for a class, you have to choose what information to include and what to exclude to fit within the time frame. During your speech, suppose that several members of the audience are nodding off. If, according to principle one, you assume responsibility for them, then you know that you have to make changes. What these changes will be requires immediate decisions on your part: lowering your voice, raising it, cutting out part of your talk, pounding the table, doing something. Then, after the talk is over, you need to think about your original planning as well as what you did during the speech. You need to reflect on what you may have forgotten to take into consideration initially and also analyze what worked. That way you incorporate what you learned into your decision making for the next talk.

## Be Aware of Your
## Strengths and Weaknesses

You should be aware of your own strengths and weaknesses as a speaker and practice those techniques that will enhance your presentation style. We all recognize that dancers, poets, athletes, and painters have talent. However, we tend to forget that to develop their talent, they have acquired and practiced techniques that enhance their innate ability. It is not sheer passion on the day that wins an Olympic Gold, nor is it merely enthusiasm that enables an actor to muster the energy for his or her 100th performance. To be successful, actors and athletes cannot rely simply on being in the mood. They have a job to do; they have years of practice and a wealth of techniques to sustain them. You, as a lecturer, as a presenter, need to understand, in the same way, that there are techniques that will enhance your skills in lecturing and in presenting. All you need to do is assess your own strengths and weaknesses and incorporate those techniques. This book is written to help show you how.

In summary, as you know, it is normal to be nervous before making a presentation, but there is no reason to be so terrified that you hurt yourself personally and professionally. You start by accepting the four basic principles explained in this chapter that are valid in the seminar room or the conference hall and that can make a difference in the quality of your presentation. Understanding and implementing these principles will start you on your way to enhancing your teaching as well as your success as a speaker.

# 2 | How We Communicate

> *How well we communicate is determined not by how well we say things, but by how well we are understood.*
> —Andrew S. Grove, CEO, Intel Corporation

Before examining in detail the techniques that will enhance your own presentation style, let's step back and examine from a theoretical perspective what happens when we communicate. This should enable you to analyze a process that is both instantaneous and taken for granted. We do not think about it. This chapter will remind you of exactly what you are doing when you speak and highlight some of the difficulties that are inherent in the process of trying to share ideas with your students, colleagues, or family. Based on a heightened awareness of the process, you should then be in a better position to assess what you can do as a speaker to minimize the difficulties and increase the odds of having your ideas understood and then acted on.

## The Communication Process

Basically, the two-way communication process requires both a sender and a receiver. Some people compare it to a tennis or ping-pong match. One author compared the communication process to the act of disassembling London Bridge in England, stone by stone, and sending it across the Atlantic to be reassembled in Arizona.

To refresh your memory, the process begins when the sender has an idea or a feeling, which is called a *message*. That message may be as simple as "Hello" or as complex as a strategic business plan or an architectural design. Regardless of its complexity or level of abstraction, it is a message that emanates from the sender and is intended for the receiver.

The next step in the process is the sender's responsibility as well. The idea or concept, the message, needs to be encoded before it is sent. There are choices of codes: words, pictures, possibly signals. For example, suppose you are the sender. You recognize a colleague in the library. You want to greet her, so you decide to encode your message with a signal, a gesture. Having made that encoding decision, you now raise your hand and transmit the greeting by moving your upraised arm quickly from side to side—you wave. But your colleague has moved into the next aisle and does not see you.

You try a different code: words, spoken words. The message remains the same, but this time you encode and transmit it in another way. The encoded message is "Hello, Ellen!," transmitted with words spoken aloud. Notice you chose to say "Hello," not "Bonjour"; you selected English, not French, when you spoke to her. But she was walking rapidly and was out of earshot, so you missed Ellen again. However, you do know her office phone number, so that afternoon you continue coding your message in English words. You phone her; she is not in, so you speak to her answering machine. This time you lengthen the message: "Hi, Ellen. Saw you in the library. Sorry I missed you. Please call me at the office." Days pass, and there is no word from Ellen. Unwilling to give up, you decide to send the message one more time, encoded again in English, but this time in writing—a note.

E. Tried to say "Hello" at the library, but missed you. Phoned on Monday, but you were out. Please call me at my extension.

The message, now longer, remains essentially "hello." You have continued to use English, but, over time, you have varied your transmission from nonverbal language, the wave, to the spoken word, both in the library and on the answering machine, and finally the written word, your letter. Sad to say, despite your efforts, Ellen still fails to respond. The critical next step in the communication process does not occur. You begin to interpret her silence as a response. Perhaps she didn't get the message, perhaps she did and chose not to answer, or perhaps there's a problem. There was a message—it was encoded in different ways and even transmitted differently, but two-way communication cannot be achieved without that next step: receipt of the message and some kind of response to it.

Good news. Nothing is amiss. Ellen finally calls you at the office and begins her conversation with "Got your letter. Sorry that I did not see you at the library and missed your call." With those words of Ellen's, you are assured that she received the message, decoded it accurately, and acted on it by doing as you asked: She phoned you.

Examined this way, communicating is a straightforward, simple process. Giving a lecture, speaking at a conference, or saying "hello" to a colleague in a library involve the same steps: identifying the message, encoding it in an appropriate language, then transmitting it so that the audience in front of you—be it 1, 5, or 500—receives your ideas, decodes them, acts or does not act on them, and gives you feedback. Simple. No problem, you say.

Sorry. There are problems—a lot of them. To be an effective speaker, you need to be sensitive to the blockages in communication, because any one of them can have significant implications for your success in having your ideas received, reflected on, or acted on. Let's look at some problems, starting as we did earlier with the initial message.

**Have a Clear Message**

Obviously, any topic that you plan to talk about is going to be far more sophisticated and complicated than "hello." Whatever the topic is, you must think the message through carefully. Even if you encode it precisely and transmit it thoughtfully, without a clear initial message your ideas may be confused. Think back to the London Bridge example. It was dismantled, sent, received, and reassembled, but the story is that the purchaser thought he was buying the Tower Bridge. The message was confused. You may have experienced this problem. You have probably walked out of a seminar room after listening to someone else's talk saying "What was that about?" or "Well, that was a waste of a morning!" or "What was the point of that?!" Those reactions suggest that the message itself was either unclear or not worthwhile to you, the listener. The lesson to you is a reminder of how important it is to think through your purpose. Chapter 6 is designed to help you refine your thinking about the intent of your own talk.

## Select Your Words Carefully

Let's assume, however, that you have worked out a clear message. Perhaps you need to explain the implications of modifying an undergraduate degree program. Sounds good. Now let's look at some encoding problems. Earlier, you decided against sending a message to Ellen in French. In that situation, the decision was easy because you knew that Ellen speaks only English. However, if you do not spend time thinking about the implications of your code choice, you can easily select an inappropriate one. To make the point, in the extreme, consider the following examples: You would most likely not translate your talk on an aspect of veterinary medicine into Latin and then intone it to the students in a Gregorian chant; an art historian would not write a comparative analysis of an artist's work in iambic pentameter; reviews of literature are not collections of photographs of book covers; and the ground staff at Chicago's O'Hare airport does not prepare a fax for a pilot to indicate where his or her aircraft should be parked.

These examples are silly, but inadvertent, silly encoding decisions are made every day. As academics, we often forget that if we decide to encode our talks in the specialized language of our fields, be it the vocabulary of medicine, geology, law, or information technology, we had best be sure that the audience knows the code. If there are members of the audience who are unfamiliar with that language, they will be unable to decipher your message. Your efforts and their time will have been wasted. Such a decision on your part would be the same as if you chose to speak Dutch to an all French-speaking audience or made reference to Maria Callas to a group more familiar with the music of "Beautiful South." In essence, you need to think hard about the choice of code.

It is not just foreign languages or technical language that can be problematic. The audience may be unable to decode what you are saying if your talk is filled with jargon. Are you throughputting, inputting, vertically challenging, synergising, or moving goal posts? Like the poor pilot at O'Hare who is waiting to park the aircraft, your audience may not be able to weigh the significance of what you are saying if they cannot decipher your meaning because of the use of specialized language, clichés, or jargon that is alien to them.

As an American, when I first walked into a shop in Ireland and was asked if I was OK, I found myself wondering whether I was looking ill. "Are you OK?" is English, but I couldn't translate what it meant in Dublin. I've learned that "Are you OK?" means "May I help you?" Years ago there was a comedy routine in a Charlie Chan film. The great detective was stopped and given a traffic ticket for making a U-turn in a one-way street. He had understood his son's words "No U-turn" to mean "No; you turn."

In other words, as a speaker you not only need to be concerned about the clarity of your initial message, but you also have to take time to be sensitive to the implications of your choice of code, if you want your message received by all as it was intended. Again, let's suppose that the message is meaningful and the code choice appropriate. What else can go wrong?

## Anticipate Transmission
## and Reception Problems:
## Human and Technical

Getting the message to the receiver can be another problem. Remember Ellen? Perhaps because of the stacks in the library, she did not hear you when you spoke, nor did she see you when you waved. You did phone her, and although you were able to leave a message on her answering machine, her line might have been busy when you called, a printer could have been on when the phone was answered, or there might be static on the line. Our poor pilot may finally get the fax with instructions about where to park, but, after all that, perhaps only the left side of it will be received—the right side is blurred.

As a speaker, you will not have to worry about answering machines or blurred faxes, but you will have to be ready to address issues like construction, disruptions, acoustic problems, microphones that do not work, the clarity of your speech pattern, your ability to project your voice in a large theater or hotel ballroom, or the quality and choice of your visuals. Anticipating and handling these problems is up to you. Remember, you have the responsibility. You are the sender. Although equipment can break down, you have control of the first steps in the communication process: the nature of the message itself, the choice of code, and the method of transmission.

## Common Problems

### Your Values

Once you have transmitted that message, you lose control of it; it moves to the receiver and therein lie more problems for you as a speaker. Suppose the receivers do not like you personally. If so, it will not make any difference what pains you take to prepare your talk; the receivers may interpret your message in terms of their perceptions of you. "There he goes, posturing again!" "Just trying to show the rest of us up." Suppose it is not your personality but your values that are annoying to the receivers. You may have a view on religion, on abortion, on homosexuality, or on the NCAA, for that matter, that the receivers find repugnant or offensive. So your message may be rejected even if the subject of your talk has nothing to do with those issues.

## Their Preoccupations

*You* may not be the problem; the receiver may be. Ellen may not have heard you in the library, not because she was out of earshot, but because she was preoccupied and concerned with the time, and she wanted to leave the building before the crush in the corridors became too heavy. In the same way, someone in your audience could be preoccupied with a personal problem, such as a large payment due on a credit card bill, a deadline for a paper that is fast approaching, or an upcoming meeting with a department head about his or her teaching load. In other words, the receiver may like you but be distracted by nonwork- or work-related issues.

## Their Minds

Let's complicate the speaking business still more. It is important to remember that the receiver—your audience—can process information more quickly than you can speak it, which means that no matter how interesting, thought provoking, or relevant the subject matter is, the receiver has the capability of listening to you and thinking about other issues at the same time: planning a vacation, thinking about lunch, picking up a video, anticipating an afternoon class, or scheduling a workshop. That ability to mentally handle more information than you can provide while speaking is a problem for you. The solution is not to speak faster to fill up the space—it is to figure out how to keep the audience's attention by being interesting.

## Your Choice of Images

Earlier there was a reference to the quality of your visuals. Let's not focus on the spoken word to the exclusion of the visual. Remember that pictures send messages and that most speakers choose to add some kind of visuals to their talks. You have undoubtedly experienced most of the encoding and transmission problems caused by visuals, because you have seen them when you were a member of an audience yourself: the print that is too small; the graph without the label; the chart with too many trends; the reprint of a page in a report; the slide with too many words; the acetate that is too big for the screen; or the picture that is blurred, distorted, or reversed—concerns, issues, worries. Maybe you have a cause to be nervous!

## Now What?

By breaking a complex process into simpler components and by highlighting some of the difficulties that may occur by looking at the problems of sending a simple greeting to a colleague, you can become more sensitive to the importance of making conscious decisions about the message, the code, and the means of transmission in advance of any lengthy talk you give. You also can see how important it is to know your receivers and why it is unwise to be overly dependent on your instincts. Communication breaks down. If you are aware of potential problems, then you can plan and organize for them. That attention to detail is one of the hallmarks of an effective speaker.

By looking at the theoretical communication model, you can begin to appreciate:

- The need to have a clear message when you speak
- The need to select your words and pictures thoughtfully
- The need to transmit what you have to say clearly
- The need to analyze your audience

Consequently, the receiver/audience will understand the implications of modifying an undergraduate degree program so clearly that you will not have 12 conversations after your talk asking you questions about what you meant. Instead, you will have conversations about your availability to speak again, more attentive students, questions about the implications of your findings, or invitations to coauthor papers.

By remembering what is involved in the two-way communication process, the mystery about speaking should disappear and your need to assume responsibility should become clearer. Your confidence and ability should increase because you will know what to do to give a good talk.

So far, our focus has been on the process of sending a message emphasizing verbal language with a brief reference to the language of images. Now, let's focus on nonverbal language as an important means of communication. It is a key element for you as an academic, because while the audience is listening to your words and looking at the slides, you and what you are doing are the focus of their attention. Frequently, what you physically do as a speaker can enhance or ruin a well-designed talk.

# 3 | Nonverbal Language

*We all, in one way or another, send our little messages to the world . . . and rarely do we send our messages consciously. We act out our state of being with nonverbal body language. We lift one eyebrow for relief. We rub our noses for puzzlement. We clasp our arms to isolate ourselves or to protect ourselves. . . . The gestures are numerous, and while some are deliberate . . . there are some that are mostly unconscious.*
— Julius Fast, author of *Body Language*

This chapter examines two main themes: (a) how your use of your body and your choice of clothing can enhance your ability to get your message across and (b) how, conversely, your body and clothing can become yet another problem in the litany of barriers that may interfere with your audience's ability to receive, decode, and react to or act on the ideas or approaches that you have labored over for days or weeks in preparation for your talk.

To increase your awareness of the impact that nonverbal language can have on your audience, the first step is to recognize the messages that certain types of body language can send to an audience and thus affect your presentation. The objective is for you to begin to identify some of your own habits. Then, pat yourself on the back for your good ones and begin to work on eliminating those gestures or actions that take away from your performance—one at a time. There may be only one, or there may be many. If the latter is the case, pick one aspect to work on at a time, then another. You will only feel frustrated if you tackle them all at once. Every weight loss diet book tells you to focus on the success of losing one pound at a time, not on the fact that you have 10 to go before you reach your desired weight. You write an article one page at a time. You teach a course one class at a time. You improve your nonverbal presentation style one aspect at a time.

Let's begin to look at some of the specific physical aspects of presentation—what the audience sees: your head, your face, your arms and hands, your gestures and stance, and your legs and your feet. Let's look at each of these to see how your use of them can interfere with your audience's ability to concentrate on your words and, at the same time, to see what you might do to reinforce your verbal message by sending appropriate nonverbal messages. Simply put, your choice or control of the physical aspects of your presentation should reinforce your message, not interfere with it. An extreme example is the habit of speaking with one hand over your mouth. You risk not being understood or heard. Some speakers actually do that and are not aware of the habit. Along the way, you may notice some of your own or other's idiosyncrasies, both positive and negative.

Please, do not berate yourself if you recognize five or six negatives. This is not a contest. To repeat, pick one and try to change that one. Then, after you have made headway, pick another one and work on it. Athletes like Shaquille O'Neal or Carl Lewis did not master all the techniques required in their respective fields in one day or one week. It takes time, effort, patience, and a pat on the back. Even if you have been lecturing for years, there is nothing wrong with giving yourself that pat.

## Your Head and Face

Let's begin at the top of your body and work down. Heads move up and down or side to side. If, as you speak, you let your head wobble, you may look like Big Bird. Suppose a female lecturer gives her talk with her head tilted to one side;

she may appear to the audience to be demure or coquettish, wistfully begging for their support or sympathy. If your talk is about the researcher's responsibility for some serious subject, and through the entire speech you have your head tilted to one side like that, with your shoulder raised to meet it, you will probably look coy or kittenish, not exactly the look for an expert in social psychology. On the other hand, if you hold your head back and your chin aloft, you may risk putting your audience off because they perceive you to be smug or arrogant.

Imagine shaking your head from side to side to signify what we in America recognize as the signal for "no," yet your words are saying "yes," how "delighted" you are to be here speaking on this occasion. Or the reverse may be true: You are shaking your head up and down to signal "yes," when you are saying that "there is definitely no correlation between . . ." In other words, unless you take care, your head may be sending one message while your words are sending another, a mixed message: "yes" with your words but "no" with your head, or "no" with your words and "yes" with your head. Literally, use your head. The way you hold it can make you appear shy or smug, when what you want is to appear confident and straightforward.

Facial expressions also can be a problem. It's remarkable the number of speakers who allow their faces to become grim when they are asked to speak to an audience, no matter what the subject. Few talks in academia are eulogies to departed colleagues. As a matter of fact, even if you were asked to give one, a eulogy can include some happy remembrances. In other words, your facial expression should reinforce your message. Sure, you are nervous about speaking, but let your face light up; try smiling or looking happy. When you say "Good morning" or "Good afternoon," a look of genuine pleasure is warranted, regardless of your initial anxiety. If you are "pleased with the outcome of the study," if you are "delighted with the recommendations," if you are "excited at the prospect," then, for heaven's sake, look pleased or delighted or excited. That does not mean that you should wear a grin from ear to ear for the duration of a class, nor should you grin if you are saying that you are "concerned" with the findings, "worried" about the quality of the research, or "disturbed" by the paucity of funding.

Once again, your face should mirror your words. Because you are likely to be nervous, you will probably have no difficulty looking worried. It is much harder to smile. But if you do, it will also help you to feel better. Try it. Don't underestimate your ability to affect those people. The warmth that you emit has an impact on the audience. Think back to how you felt when you walked into school when you were a child. In one room you were greeted by a smiling teacher and in another by a tight-lipped snarler. Know that you can produce the same feelings in your students that were produced in you. You can affect their level of interest or motivation by exuding a feeling of warmth or by looking cold and distant. Smiles work wonders. In retrospect, I can still recall my dread when I encountered those cold, distant, and stern teachers. (Not that sometimes those looks were not warranted.)

## Your Eyes

Now that you are holding your head up and smiling sometimes, what about those eyes of yours? Yes, everyone knows to make eye contact. Do you really understand why? Do you genuinely look at people and, more important, do you see what you are looking at—really see what's before you? You should be looking at every face in the audience, not talking over their heads or out of the window, or intoning into the upper left-hand corner of the room. No matter how many are in the room, you should look at each and every face and see the reactions to your words.

The reasons are twofold: (a) By looking at each face, you are signaling to the audience that you like them, that you have nothing to hide, and that you are honest, open, and direct; and (b) by looking at *and* seeing those faces and reactions, you are also able to get some immediate feedback for you to react to—a critical dimension in the two-way communication process—unlike Ellen in the previous chapter who didn't give us feedback until she finally returned the call, thus leaving us wondering why or what to do.

In Chapter 4, you will learn what to do with what you see. For the moment, let's stay with the looking. When you look at everyone, do not start at the left side of the room and move your eyes methodically to the right, or start at the right side and then move your eyes to the left and then back to the right like a periscope in search of a target.

Look at everyone randomly. "Everyone" means just that, not only the person whom you perceive to be a power figure in the room—the one with the title or the responsibility. Even Don Corleone had a consigliere. In other words, be careful not to assume that all decisions are made unilaterally by the dean, the president, the chair, the department head, or the conference coordinator. People in power seek advice from different people, and those people may be there as well.

Another good reason for looking at faces is that when you look at someone, that person will usually return the glance. Thus, rather than thinking about the credit card bill, or the next class, people pay attention. In addition, you are sending the message with your eyes that you value everyone in the room. Everyone is important. Please do not have staring contests; a few seconds on a face is enough. One caveat though: Watch out for the "nodder." There is always someone in the room who is hanging on your every word and nodding in agreement with every word you say—a friend, a disciple. Thank goodness! But do not be misled. You are nervous, so it's natural for you to be grateful for some reassurance. As a speaker, when you are feeling vulnerable, it is easy to lock your eyes onto that nodding head like a guided missile. Soon you will find that you are directing your talk only to that individual, to the neglect of the others in the room. One lecturer tells a story of doing just that only to discover that the nodding head was not in agreement with his words of wisdom but rather in response to the beat of the music emanating from the student's head-phones. Therefore, although you may have successfully devel-oped a relationship with one person, the others may stop listening and may even resent your neglect. The audience may have similar feelings if you speak predominantly to one side of the room, perhaps because more people are seated on the left or on the right. Catch yourself if you do, and work to correct that tendency so that you involve everyone.

## Your Body

What about those appendages that are connected to your shoulders—your arms? And those additional bits at the end—your hands? What a nuisance they are for a speaker! Where did they come from, you ask, and, worse yet, what do you do with them? Just as you have seen poor visuals, you have also witnessed all the attempts by speakers to solve the arm-hand problem. Can you remember them?

- Some speakers glue their arms to their sides and look like telephone or totem poles.
- Some speakers rid themselves of the darn things by clasping them behind their backs.
- Some speakers wish to appear nonchalant and seek to do so by putting one hand in a pocket or sometimes one hand in each pocket. Sometimes the speaker forgets and begins to play with the 57 cents in a pocket—another noisy distraction.
- Some speakers take a more defensive posture and cross their arms on their chests. A variation would be crossing the arms with the hands held together as if in prayer. The speaker not only appears to be fending off attack but also appears to be seeking divine intervention. Whereas some seek to protect the vulner-able upper body, others, perhaps because of a healthy knowl-edge of the perils of sport, protect themselves lower down.

None of these solutions is ideal. What happens is that instead of looking open and confident, you may appear to the audience to be stiff, insecure, scared, or defensive. The truth is that you may feel that way, but you should not shout it at your audience with a nonverbal message when you want your verbal message to sound strong, open, and honest.

So, what do you do? First of all, remember that nonverbal language should reinforce your verbal message, not contradict or undermine it. In effect, you are a living visual. Your head, hands, and arms can all be used to assist you in communicating your ideas. Although it takes practice to unglue that arm from your side or to take one hand out of a pocket, try to use them and move them just the way that you do when you are having a conversation with a colleague or student.

To become more self-aware, have a conversation with a friend and notice how both of you use your hands to make a point or to clarify a concept. Notice how useful your fingers are for counting or for making points: "The three concerns . . ." or "Two reasons why . . ." In formal speaking, be careful not to script your movements; that is, do not decide in advance to touch your chest every time you use the word "I" or point to the audience every time you say "you." You will begin to look like a marionette. Try to talk conversationally and use your hands naturally. For example, if something you are describing is large, show how large with your hands; if it is heavy, heft it. How do people describe the size of the lobster they ate? With their hands. Be careful, though, of wringing your hands, particularly when the subject of your talk is financial. Rather than appearing to be an educator, you may look like Fagin. Avoid pointing at the audience under any circumstance, with your finger, with a pen, or with a pointer. It is a threatening gesture and may offend them. I recall working with a lecturer who used a pointer that was at least 6 feet long. He looked like a knight. No one in the audience was prepared to question his authority. Try to use an open, whole hand, not just your index finger poking at your audience as if you were prodding the bad guy's chest or aiming a gun at him.

Again, use your entire body to reinforce your message and to emphasize your points, not to confuse or distract your audience. That point is equally true of your legs, your feet, and your stance. Unless you are an actor in a grade B cowboy movie, try to keep both hips even, not one up and one down.

Do keep them even. When you walk up to the front of the room or the platform, stand with assurance. Plant each foot in a line directly below each of your shoulders to support your weight evenly. If you stand with your feet pressed together, you may appear to be on the verge of toppling over, and your audience might very well be waiting for you to do just that. They'll no longer concentrate on your words. Do you take dance positions with your feet or actually begin to dance the tango or cha-cha? Some speakers rock from side to side or roll up and down on their toes. Don't. Still others cross their ankles while they are standing or bend their ankles as if they were just learning to ice skate. Remember, you want to appear strong, open, and confident, not like the Leaning Tower of Pisa or an extra in an early Clint Eastwood western, with your hips and shoulders akimbo, hands in the pocket. Again, the risk is that the focus of attention shifts from your ideas to the image you are creating.

Don't be reluctant to move around. You should feel free to walk normally and confidently, not in mincing steps like a caged animal pacing in a tight space, but really moving. Speak from the right, move to the left, if it is appropriate or warranted. There are no rules against moving so long as you do so with clear purpose. Of course, if you are working with a fixed microphone in a large room, your options are more limited. You may want to ask if other kinds of mikes are available, because movement creates interest and energizes your talk. However, don't forget to maintain eye contact as you move.

By the way, there are added benefits to standing up straight, with chest up and shoulders relaxed. Your voice will be stronger, and you will be able to maintain eye contact better. It is easy to lean on furniture, to welcome any kind of support, even if it is from a wooden dais. But if you do, you will look tired or lazy, casual or frightened, so try to avoid holding onto desks or lecterns or leaning against furniture. By the way, when a big man with a big voice leans toward the audience he can appear threatening. Stand tall and look open. Your heart may be pounding, but you will look and sound self-assured. There are times in small group settings that you may choose to sit in a chair or on a table; however, even then you may elect to stand from time to time, so you should be sensitive to your visual impact.

There is another category of nonverbal messages: idiosyncratic gestures. You need to discover whether you have any particular gestures that are distracting, like repeatedly putting that stray length of hair behind your ear, frequently tossing your head to get the bangs out of your eyes, pushing your glasses up onto your nose, scratching your head, or pulling your ear. There is nothing inherently wrong with any of these gestures. You are human, after all, and they are normal, but when any one movement is repeated so often that the audience begins to notice it, problems arise. What happens is that your listeners begin to pay more attention to the frequency with which you straighten your tie, fix your hair, or push your glasses up on your nose than they do to your interpretations of Yeats's poetry. Not too long ago, I watched an audience become transfixed by a speaker's nervous rubbing of his cheek. His words and, therefore, his efforts were lost.

## Your Clothing

It is time to talk about your choice of clothing. If you think of presenting in terms of the theater world, then consider your clothes as your costume. They need to be selected with care. They should match the occasion, whether it is a weekend retreat that is casual or a formal presentation to corporate executives. All of you, the whole package, is under scrutiny: what you say, how you use your body, and what you wear.

Again, you do not want to create unnecessary distractions. No, it is not that the audience will notice brown buttons or black ones, but they may notice unpolished shoes. They may focus on the holes in your socks, the worn-down heels, or the runs in stockings. You risk the audience thinking that if you are sloppy about those details, perhaps you will be sloppy about the ideas that you are discussing as well. I remember seeing a speaker wearing an overcoat during a talk. Yes, the room was cold, but afterward the topic of conversation was not about what she was saying but why she was in a hurry to leave, and the people milling about wondered whether or not she was interested in speaking on that occasion. In other words, the audience wants to feel as if they are important to you.

In addition to wearing something appropriate, choose something comfortable. That does not mean your gardening or biking clothes. Because of all that you have on your mind, select clothing that is going to be problem-free: no tight collars, no shoes that pinch, no buttons that open unexpectedly, no scarves that slide off, and no skirts that ride up. In other words, the fewer unnecessary concerns you have, the better your talk is likely to be.

Select the clothing that looks best on you and fits you well. Pass up the trousers with the cuffs that bunch around your ankles or the jacket that looks like it belongs to someone taller or shorter. For men, be sure that the collar of the shirt closes and fits you at the neck. Lost any buttons? Replace them. If you are wearing a tie, select one that remains knotted and that will stay comfortably at the neck to cover that collar button. Before you get up to speak, straighten that tie and do it just once. Just like fixing your hair or playing with your glasses, repeated tie fixing is a distraction. Forgive the familiarity, but are your trousers around your waist? Or are you hiking them up several times? Perhaps suspenders or a tighter belt is in order.

What colors to select? What styles to wear? Those are your decisions to make as well. You know what makes you look good. There are books on the subject of color and style for your skin tone and build. There are certain fashions and colors that look better on some people. Decide whether a double-breasted suit is the most flattering for your height and weight. Why select an outfit that is in fashion but that makes you look shorter or heavier than you are? If you are not built for the latest design, go for a classic look and hold out for the style to change. If purple is this year's color but it is not yours, select the one that looks good on you. Pale yellow or green makes *me* look as though a trip to the doctor's office is in order. High contrast (e.g., black against white or navy against white) or charcoal gray against a light background give you an image of higher authority. Think about where you have seen those color combinations worn. Blue against yellow or beige against yellow are softer, friendlier combinations. Maybe you should consider wearing brighter colors on drearier days, for the class on Tuesday after Labor Day, or on a Monday morning. In other words, your choice of clothing is another important decision for you to make. Having taken so much trouble to look good, beware! If a meal precedes your talk, consider carefully what you choose to eat. On one hand, depending on your nerves, a light meal instead of liver and onions or hot chili may be easier on your stomach; you don't need to be reminded of what you ate halfway through the talk. On the other hand, the audience does not need to know that you ate spaghetti and meat sauce because they see a spot on your blouse or shirt.

Finding the right "costume" may be harder for women than for men, who usually do not have to make as many choices about what to wear. Your decision should be governed by the words, "appropriate for the occasion," that is, long skirt, short skirt, slacks, pant suit, slit skirt, and so on. The fuchsia mohair sweater, the see-through blouse with the décolletage, the three-inch earrings, or the skirt "for standing only" may not be right for the occasion. Each item in and of itself may be stunning on you, but if you are delivering a serious message that has implications for you or for the college or university that you represent, you need to ensure that the audience is focused on your face, your words, your visuals, and your message, not on how stunning you are or what a great figure you have. No, you do not need to wear a three-piece suit. If in doubt, lean to the conservative. Finally, choose comfortable shoes.

You look good. You have selected comfortable, appropriate clothes that do not distract. Make one more decision: how to wear your hair. Is your hair in your eyes? Are the bangs too long? I have seen both men and women who appear to have only one eye or who expend valuable energy fighting independent strands of hair that keep falling out of place and annoying them and, by so doing, interfere with the audience's ability to concentrate on the words.

Finally, wear a watch. The room you are working in may not have a clock, so you may need to keep an eye on your time, particularly if you are speaking at a tightly scheduled conference.

You can see that in addition to content, there is much to think about when you speak. You are sending nonverbal messages along with your verbal ones, so you should become more aware of how you use your body, your head, your face, and your arms and hands; the way you stand and move; and, then, how you choose to dress on the day. There are no absolutes, no rules, but remember to make conscious decisions all the time. Don't leave it all up to chance. For any number of reasons, you may decide that you are deliberately not going to smile; that you want to take off your jacket and roll up your sleeves; that you think it's advisable to sit on the table or to wear a tie that looks like a fish or the stockings with sequins at the ankles. If you do, you presumably have decided that doing any or all of these things will have the impact that you want to have on your audience and that it will ultimately send them on their way remembering your message.

# 4 | Voice and Speech Patterns

*Proper words in proper places, make the true definition of a style.*
—Jonathan Swift

By now you are probably wondering how you are ever going to remember all this advice—look pleasant, but not all of the time; look at people's faces, but not for too long; use your hands to emphasize points, but not too often; stand tall and walk around, but do not pace. You haven't even begun to organize the content yet. Before you can do the drafting, however, it is important to examine two more physical aspects of presentation: your voice and speech pattern, and the impact they can have on your audience.

Many speakers take their voices for granted. In fact, by not taking full advantage of what your voice can do, you undervalue it. Sure, you could take speech or elocution lessons, but there is much that you can do on your own to improve the use of your voice and to modify your speech. As with correcting inappropriate body language, the first step in the process of enhancing your vocal quality involves awareness, recognizing what you can do with your voice and speech pattern to take advantage of their potential for turning an OK talk into an excellent one. Let's examine several aspects of speaking: pacing, pausing, accents, pitch, volume, projection, extraneous sounds or words, clarity, and emphasis.

## Pacing

We'll begin with the speed at which you talk, the *pace*. If you learn to accelerate and decelerate, you are well on your way to enhancing your delivery, because pacing is, in fact, one of the biggest stumbling blocks for the less seasoned speaker. There is good reason for this. Most of us tend to speak too quickly when we initially stand up to talk in front of a group. Why? In part because most of us speak more quickly when we are nervous, and being nervous makes us want to get the ordeal over with as quickly as possible. We rush, but if you remember the responsibility that you have to your audience, you realize that you can't race through your talk. The audience needs to be able to comprehend what you are saying. When you speak at a conference or to 300 students in a lecture hall, unlike participating in a seminar, for instance, the members of the audience are not in a position to engage you in conversation or to say "Would you mind clarifying that last point?" or "Did I understand you to mean . . .?" They are dependent on how you say what you say. Therefore, you need to speak slowly enough for everyone to capture your message without an opportunity to ask you questions.

Because you are likely to be more nervous at the beginning of a talk than at the end of it, overcompensate for that nervousness by speaking your opening sentences slowly, ensuring that your first words do not all run together. Have you ever heard someone open a talk with "Goodmorningit'snicetoseeyou"? If that sounds like what it looks like, one word, it will be hard to understand, and those people facing you will concentrate at first, but they may expend less effort trying to follow you after a while. You've seen it; the eyes will glaze over or shut altogether. Others will appear to be listening but will really be thinking of other things that they have to do.

## Pausing

Pausing is an option that we often forget. Frequently, in their eagerness to be done, speakers race through the entire talk like an express train. Consider taking a more leisurely route; make some local stops. Speed up through less important material, slow down through the nuts and bolts. And pause. Pick your moments, of course. Pausing is an excellent technique because an occasional silence gives the audience a chance to take in your words, to absorb them, perhaps to reflect on them. For example, speakers frequently build rhetorical questions into their talks: "Why should you be concerned with . . . ?" But rather than wait, they charge ahead. They do not give the audience time to think, either about the question or about a possible answer. Another instance is when the speaker has decided to startle the audience with a new concept. Let's suppose it's a proposal for the introduction of a new degree program. Rather than making the initial recommendation for the new program and then pausing to permit the audience to get their heads around the idea, the speaker proceeds into four justifications and six implications for the recommendation— each one of which may require some thought. While you are making point number nine, the audience may still be thinking about the implications of the original notion—a new degree.

Sometimes a pause also benefits you, the *presenter*. You can take a sip from a glass of water, collect your thoughts, or find your place in your notes. Another reason for pausing might be that you want to allow the audience to have the opportunity to jot down some notes or salient questions as you speak. They will not be able to write anything if you are already talking about justification number four and if they are still processing numbers two and three. You have seen it happen in class. You ask if there are any questions, hoping for some insight, and hear, "What was number three?" So, take appropriate pauses.

To repeat: slow down, particularly at the beginning, but also throughout the talk when you are establishing your key points. Consider varying the pace, sometimes slow, sometimes fast, and sometimes pausing or even stopping altogether, not just for the sake of pausing or stopping, but because doing so alters the impact of your talk and allows the audience time to reflect on your ideas. Just like physical movement, vocal variation makes the talk more interesting to listen to, thus helping to eliminate one of our concerns about being boring.

## Accents

Suppose you come from another part of the city, the country, or the world than where you are speaking—born in Memphis, speaking in London. You may pronounce words in ways that are unfamiliar to most of the audience, a concern that is more real in an age of international symposia or visiting lectureships. If attendees are unused to certain sounds, they may have difficulty decoding at first, so, once again, take your time. Give the audience a chance to adjust to the way you pronounce certain sounds. They will adjust in time. People who have heavy regional accents are often advised to rid themselves of them. If you have one but are understood by others, don't change. Audiences welcome the difference. If, however, you discover that a particular sound you make confuses or changes the meaning of what you are saying, then work on that single sound. For example, you may want to avoid puzzling your audience as to whether you said "three" or "tree" or "pin" or "pen."

## Pitch

You are also more interesting to listen to if you vary the pitch of your voice. The word "monotone" means just that—one sound. Your voice, like a musical instrument, has a range. By learning to raise or lower the pitch, you can avoid that "poor-Johnny-one-note" quality. Just as singers have ranges, so do we as speakers. What happens when you ask a question? Your voice invariably goes up at the end of a sentence to signal to the listener that you are asking a question. This suggests that you are capable of varying the pitch. Isn't that so? If you say that last sentence aloud, notice the variation in pitch. Record your voice, listen to the musical quality that you have, and consider varying the pitch as you speak; again, like adjusting the pace, the change avoids the potential for droning that we have all heard, endured, and dread.

## Volume

Now, let's add volume to our list of variables. You may be beginning to feel like a CD player. You know very well that you are capable of speaking softly or loudly as well as somewhere in between, because, on one hand, you have all whispered to a colleague sitting next to you at a meeting, and, on the other, you have also shouted with pleasure or dismay during a game. In other words, you raise and lower the volume all the time. Remember to do that when you give a talk; add that ability to the rest of your repertoire of talents. The options for creating verbal diversity, and thus interest, are increasing. "But I always speak softly," you say. Just slow down and stand tall, look out, breathe deeply, and project your voice to the back of the room, not down at the table in front of you or, like the elementary school poem reciter, to the floor. You *will* be heard.

## Projection

In the previous chapter, maintaining eye contact was mentioned as an important skill to develop. There was a reference both to looking at the audience and to seeing their reactions. What follows is an example of the importance of seeing what your audience is doing. It also illustrates why, though we are looking at presentation in bits and pieces, it also needs to be viewed as a whole. How many times have you heard a speaker ask the question, "Can you hear me in the back?" Why, oh why, do speakers ask it? Courtesy? It is a silly question. But the problem it raises is a serious one: How can you be sure that those in the back of the room *can* hear you?

If you are speaking in a large room and prefer to work without a microphone and you are worried about not being heard, one technique is to imagine that aging relatives are seated in the back row, that their hearing is not what it was, and that none of them is wearing a hearing aid. Project your voice to the back and direct your opening remarks to them. When you speak your first sentences, look at those people and see their reactions. You will quickly discover whether they can or cannot hear you without having to ask. How do you know? Watch *their* nonverbal language. They will send a message back to you. They may lean toward you or turn their heads so that their ears are directed toward you, suggesting that they are straining to hear, or the looks on their faces will show their reactions to what you have said, thus indicating that they can hear you. In other words, there is no need to ask "Can you hear me in the back?" You can read the reaction without asking. Furthermore, what would their usual answer be in any case? "No" means that they heard you ask the question, and "Yes" means that they heard you as well. All the speaker has succeeded in doing by asking the question, therefore, is to disrupt the flow of the talk, particularly at that critical starting point. Then again, asking "Can you hear me in the back?" may be a great opening if "Hearing and Listening" is your topic for the day's talk. Particularly in the early stages of your talk, therefore, in addition to making a conscious effort to adjust your volume, pace, and pitch, project your voice to the back row and check the reactions.

## Extraneous Sounds or Words

Some of us make unnecessary sounds or use unnecessary words when we speak. To discover if *you* do, you may want to seek the help of a colleague or use a cassette player or tape recorder. Speak to your colleague or into the machine on any subject for a few minutes. Play back the recording or have your friend give you feedback. Your goal is to discover if you are making any extraneous sounds. For example, you may not realize that you have the habit of saying "um" or "er" between words when you pause. You may make "tsk" or clicking sounds because of the way you press your tongue against the roof of your mouth. You may smack your lips. No, it is certainly not the end of the world if you do make any or all of those sounds, but, like the other physical aspects of presentation, too many "ums" or "tsks" will be distracting. Watch pet words or phrases as well. Sometimes speakers begin sentences with "well" or "right" or end them with "you know" or "OK." Students have been known to bet on the frequency of the repetition of those words during a lecture. Clearly, content is lost under those circumstances.

What do you do to stop? First, become aware of the habit, then catch yourself in the act and try to avoid it the next time you do it. You will, though not every time. Slowly and steadily the sounds will disappear, and you will replace the old habit with a new one—silence between words.

Besides making "tsk" and "um" sounds, some speakers actually "sigh" when they talk. Have you ever spoken to anyone who yawns on the phone? That inhalation and expulsion of a deep breath sounds sad, pitiful, or bored. "Poor me," it says. It does little to assist you in motivating your audience about a new concept or challenging project. Again, how do you stop? Just catch yourself. Remember that the first step in ridding yourself of these little mannerisms is awareness.

## Clarity

If you decide to record your own voice, also listen for clarity in your speech. Do your words have endings? Can you hear the final letters, the "s," "ing," "d," and the "t"? If you cannot hear them, it is possible that you may be slurring your words, which may cause the audience difficulty in deciphering your meaning. Does it sound like "Goomorninisnicetobespeakinin-Detroitoday"? Simply slow down and practice saying the ends of your words. A colleague in the theater arts or media center may have exercises you can use, or you can make your own like repeating "she sells seashells by the seashore" or finding lines from poems or plays that you can practice: "Friends, Romans, Countrymen, lend me your ears."

## Emphasis

There is another variable that you should consider in addition to pitch, pace, volume, or clarity—it is emphasis. The best way to illustrate how emphasis can enhance a talk is to let you experiment. Read each of the following sentences, emphasizing the italicized part:

> *I* am delighted to be here today.
> I *am* delighted to be here today.
> I am *delighted* to be here today.
> I am delighted to be *here* today.
> I am delighted to be here *today*.
> *I am delighted* / to be here today.
> I am delighted / *to be here today*.

By changing the emphasis, you change the meaning of the sentence. Think about what's important when you are practicing your talk and when you deliver it. Decide whether there are key phrases or words that will enhance your message if you literally underline them with your voice. Please do not overrehearse. You'll begin to sound like a Stepford Wife or a robot, not a human being. Remember the earlier recommendation; effective speakers make decisions—before, *during*, and after, not all in advance of the talk.

In other words, when you are sending your message to the audience, what you do with your voice and speech will assist you in ensuring that your talk is both heard and interesting to listen to. Don't underestimate the number of variables you have to play with. Therefore, remember to do the following:

- Vary the pace to maintain interest.
- Pause to allow the audience to take in your ideas.
- Adjust your accent only if a sound you utter confuses the meaning of your words. Accents create diversity.
- Like pacing, varying the pitch creates interest.
- Adjust the volume of your voice throughout your talk, both to be heard and to avoid monotony.
- Project your voice to the back row.
- Eliminate any extraneous sounds like "ems" and "ers" or words like "you know" or "OK."
- Check to see if your word endings are clearly enunciated.
- Decide which words or phrases should be emphasized to press home your point.

# 5 | Getting Ready

*I keep six honest serving men.*
*They taught me all I knew:*
*Their names are What and Why and When*
*and How and Where and Who.*

—Rudyard Kipling

So far, you have been reminded of what is involved in the two-way communication process and its inherent problems. You also are becoming more conscious of the implications of the physical aspects of presenting. Now it is time to look at the questions that you need to ask once you have been invited to speak at a conference or intend to speak at a seminar or meeting or to organize a class. Once you have the answers to your questions, you will be more in control and thus be able to enhance your professional image, as well as your confidence. You will have fewer surprises. Furthermore, some of the answers to these questions will aid you in making some essential decisions in advance of the event, about what you are going to say and how you are going to say it.

What are these questions? No surprise. They are Kipling's six men: where, when, who, what, why, and how. I hope that scholars will forgive the presumption of my expanding on his famous maxim by adding four more: why me, how long, who else, and how many. Although we will look at each question individually, every one is, in fact, another thread that forms the tapestry of your talk. Let's examine each question to understand, first, what you want to learn by asking it, and, second, what implications the answers have for your decision making and therefore for your presentation.

## "Why Me?"

This question is critical because it seeks to determine why you and not someone else has been selected to speak. More often than not, the answer to this question should build your confidence and thus assist in settling your nerves. More than likely the question will elicit responses such as "You are the best person to do it"; "You have been closest to the research," which suggests that you "know your stuff"; "You are a splendid presenter"; or "You were excellent at the _____ conference," which is always nice to hear. If, in a worst case scenario, you are told, "No one else wants to do it," you can still be pleased because the selector believes that you have the ability to give the talk. Consequently, the answer to "why me?" should replace some of your self-doubts with more positive notions about your competence or style.

## "How Long?"

Reassurances aside, it is time to plan. What you want to know is how much time the talk should take, including or in addition to any question time. The answer to the question "how long?" will tell you if the talk is to be 10 minutes, 15 minutes, or 25 minutes. Pin it down. Is it 15 minutes, plus 10 minutes for questions, a total of 25? Or is it 5 minutes with 10 minutes of questioning, a total of 15? Or is it 15 minutes with no questions? The answer may be that no one has considered the issue yet. Press the point, and make a recommendation or a decision. As you well know, the length of time you have to talk has critical implications for what you select for the content. Whether you have 15 or 25 minutes to talk about the future directions of the field will mean that the degree of detail you can include will vary enormously. Then again, are you going to lecture or read *at* the audience for 25 minutes or will you be expected to or want to involve them in some way?

You know from your classroom experience that the business of time is important. The amount of time you have to speak amounts to a contract with the audience. Some speakers forget. When you ask "how long," you must honor the answer. Ten minutes is 10 minutes, not 15. Twenty-five minutes is not 35 minutes. You know how you feel when you have a 10:30 appointment somewhere and are kept waiting until 11:00. Everyone responsible for that delay was, I am sure, apologetic, but how did you feel? Annoyed? Angry? Impatient? Frustrated? Kicking yourself for being on time? Thinking about what else you might be doing besides reading old copies of *Time* or *National Geographic?* You elicit exactly the same feelings in others when you speak longer than they expect you to. Remember your responsibility to your audience. They also have other meetings to attend and duties to perform. Of course, if you are invited to continue beyond the time, fine, but plan to say what has to be said in the time allotted. Worse yet is when you are one of a series of speakers at a conference or on a panel and each one runs 3 or 4 minutes longer than planned. Suppose you are scheduled as the last one before the lunch break. Think about it. Will stomachs rumble and lunch be delayed because you had to start late, or will you find yourself being asked to cut out 10 minutes of your talk as I once had to because the caterers were scheduled to serve at 12:30 on the dot? Enough said! Watch the time!

### "Who Else?"

What this question seeks to elicit is whether there will be any other people speaking. If so, who, about what, and in what sequence? The answer again assists you in the selection of content. Be sure to request the time slot that you want. If you learn that, yes, the university president will be speaking or the academic vice president or that a world-renowned business leader or entertainer is keynoting, you may not want to be the next speaker on the program. Although it is not always possible to do, try to find out the sequence of speakers and decide where you want to be placed in relation to each of them. In addition to who they are, what they are expected to talk about is equally important for you to know. For example, it is helpful to know in advance that Professor X will be emphasizing the importance of effective teaching in universities, particularly if the subject of your talk is emphasizing the importance of research. In other words, if it is possible, be aware of the other speakers' perspectives on a subject. Having this kind of information in advance will help you include or exclude material, underline certain concepts, or incorporate the philosophical positions of your cospeakers into your talk (e.g., "Whereas Professor X views teaching as critical, we must not forget the vital place that research . . .").

## "How Many?"

You are asking this question to help you determine your presentational style and perhaps the design of your talk as well. Typically, the larger the group, the more formal you tend to be. As you well know from lecturing, it is possible, but more difficult, to be casual and interactive with 250 people in the room. By learning how many will attend you can also think about the type of visuals or handouts that you might need for those numbers and plan what you will need designed, typed, or photocopied. Maybe a whiteboard or flip chart will be sufficient with 5 people, whereas slides or other electronic media might be necessary for 200. Remember, do not take action yet. You are merely asking questions to collect data to help you make sensible decisions about your talk.

## "Where?"

This question seeks to determine both the general location of the venue and the specific room within it that is intended to be used for your talk. Learning that the talk is to be given in the boardroom in the administration building requires one kind of reconnaissance, but learning that the talk is to be given in the ballroom at a hotel in Atlanta or Boston when you work in Des Moines, another type is required. Naturally, if the event is off-campus and you have to travel some distance to get there, then there is additional time required for acclimatization and to ensure that you or the organizers will have the equipment that you need. If the presentation is in your university's boardroom, preparations will probably be less complicated, but you will still have to get to know the room, its strengths, and limitations. Chapter 11 addresses in detail the importance of getting to know the idiosyncrasies of the room.

## "When?"

As with the other questions, this one seeks more than one piece of information. On one hand, you want to know the date of your talk so that you can determine how much time you have to get organized—2 weeks, a month, tomorrow at 10:00 a.m.? In fact, based on what you hear, you may decide to say that you cannot do it. In a situation where you have too little time to prepare, you may want to decline.

Time constraints may affect the quality of your talk. Remember that your good name is at stake, so the right decision is to say "no." However, sometimes you can influence someone else's decision. Negotiate. "Tuesday is not possible, but Thursday is." Whenever possible make choices about the timing that work for you. Naturally, if you are asked to speak at a faculty meeting that is scheduled for the third Thursday of every month, you will probably have no choice, but when you have options, take them. That's true not only for the day of the week but also, perhaps more important, for the time of day.

For example, are you being asked to speak right after lunch? Do you want to? Analyze your working style. Do you concentrate better in the morning, therefore, are you a morning person? Do you feel more alert at 9:00 a.m. than at 3:00 p.m., or is the reverse true? Request the time slot that works for you. If you are identified as a dynamic speaker, you may find yourself slotted in the tough after-lunch spot. Don't agree to it, unless you want to be there. In other words, find out as much as you can by asking "when," not only because of the implications the answer has for you personally but also because there may be design implications. Do you think that the mood of the audience on Tuesday morning after a long weekend will be the same as on a Friday afternoon? You know how you feel in such a circumstance. Will you be speaking at the same time as a play-off game broadcast, an inaugural address, the final heats of the Olympics, an election, or the Academy or Grammy Awards? Will the cold of winter or the brilliance of a summer day affect the motivation of the group before you? When you know *when*, you then should analyze what may interfere with your talk being received by the audience or what you have to take into consideration in order to have your message taken seriously.

## "Who?"

Because of the emphasis that I place on the importance of the audience, you already know that this is a key question. Remember the two-way communication process. The answer to "who" is going to assist you in understanding more about the receivers of your message and, therefore, what kind of codes should be selected for them. The answer to your question "how many" has already given you the number in attendance. Now you are looking for more specific information about those individuals. Important in the university setting, it becomes even more important when your audience is drawn from a variety of sectors. One faux pas can alienate the entire group.

Therefore, on one level, a demographic breakdown helps. What are the sex, age, education, nationality, and work experience of the audience? What is their native language? Will there be simultaneous or sequential translation? What are their job titles, what types of organizations or departments are they working in, or what kinds of organizations do they belong to or represent—private, public, large, small, educational, business, profit, or nonprofit? All of this kind of information is important whether the talk is being delivered within your own university or at an international conference. Naturally, if it is at home you will be more familiar with your own colleagues, but, even so, remember to ask who is going to be there: Heads of departments? Your immediate colleagues? Teaching assistants? Administration? Support services? Students? Only the psychology department? You are looking for their perspectives on the subject matter and their level of knowledge about your topic to determine what you can assume or have to explain.

Try to find out some of the internal politics that might affect the group dynamics or the questions. Who has just been promoted? Whose promotion was denied? Who is counting the days to retirement? Who was asked to attend but does not want to? Who is hostile? Who is looking for funding? In other words, the more you know about the group, the more accurately you will be able to select the appropriate data and anecdotes for your talk. You will also be able to cover quickly what you believe is known by all. For example, if everyone has been in college teaching or working in the university for 5 years or more, you may have to provide only a cursory review of the background of your topic. If the group coming is composed of students from varied backgrounds or experience, you may decide to devote more time explaining the context of the talk, but at the expense of something else, if time is limited. Suppose your talk is primarily about the findings from some of your recent research. To ensure understanding, it is helpful to know what your audience's comfort level is with certain terminology or current concepts in the field. Naturally, if they are unfamiliar with the subject, you may need to include essential definitions of terms.

Just as you do in your classroom, what you are doing is constantly seeking data to determine what your audience already knows and what you will need to explain in order for them to understand a given topic. In addition, you will also be determining their level of interest. For example, if you discover by questioning that everyone is required to attend the meeting, you may have a different motivational task than if you learn that they all opted to attend.

"Why all the demographic stuff?" you may ask. As you will see in Chapter 6, an effective talk is filled with real-life examples, images, and anecdotes. Therefore, the more you know about the audience, the more accurate you can be in selecting these analogies. Given what you know about a group's age, sex, job title, or place of birth, you will be in a better position to decide if you can refer to Madonna, Maureen O'Hara, BMWs, Le Mans, Grunge, Clarence Darrow, Senator Packwood, marketshare, River Phoenix, Mario Cuomo, a huddle, a base hit, tennis, knitting, or cooking. Will they know what or whom you are talking about when you make reference to such illustrations? Will the reference clarify or confound?

### "What?"

This question concerns the content of your talk. When you ask "what," the answer should clarify the theme, the content, and the subject matter of your talk. Of course, the scope or depth of the talk will be affected by the amount of time you have to talk. Are you supposed to critique the recent articles on a new scientific approach in your field, or the two most recent ones in the latest journals? Or are you to discuss one argument for or against that new approach? If you learn that you are to explain a new procedure, are you expected to include the rationale for the policy as well as the implementation, or are you only being asked to explain the nature of the procedure itself? In other words, the question "what" sets the parameters of the talk. Until you have a complete answer to this question, though, your talk will have little impact or none at all.

## "Why?"

This question goes beyond the content. It is essential to ask it so that you can determine the purpose of the talk. It is the question least often asked. Suppose the answer to your "what" question was to talk about the state of the current research in your field. The next question, "why," seeks to determine a rationale for the audience's needing or wanting to know about that research. In other words, you as a speaker have to articulate what is in it for them as a result of what you are telling them. As difficult as it might be, you will hold the audience's attention if you can convince them that what you are saying is useful and applicable to them.

For example, do you want them to understand a new grading policy in order to avoid some kind of confusion? Do you want them simply to understand that there is a new policy? Do you want them to understand that there are grave implications if there are violations of the policy? Do you want them to understand those implications? Do you want them not to be concerned by the change of policy? Therefore, is the purpose to show how the new policy is not so different from the old one? Do you want them to see the benefits of the policy? Do you want to tell them about the new policy, so that they will be more accepting of it now that they have been invited to have information shared with them? Are they there to vote on the new policy? Or are they there to debate it? Too often, audience's minds wander because as intriguing as the topic may sound or how professionally it is delivered, the speaker has not taken the time to think about why it is relevant.

In essence, your question "why" is asked to ensure that you and the audience know what the point of the talk is. It is your responsibility as a speaker to ensure that the audience knows why they are there and that they understand your point. They may not like the implications of what they are hearing, but, if you have prepared well, they will understand what you have said and why they heard it.

## "How?"

This question seeks to determine the best method for making the presentation. Perhaps the person who nominated you as the speaker already has a plan in mind. Is it to be a panel discussion? But given the issue, the time, and the audience, would a question-and-answer approach be better? Are you being asked to speak for 20 minutes? Are you supposed to read a paper for 35 minutes? Some plans may already be in place, but, given the answers you have received to your questions about what, why, and who, you may decide that the initial design will not work or be as effective; it may be boring, too structured, too interactive, or too casual. You can see that although each one of these questions is separate, they are all interrelated. Talking for 45 minutes to 100 senior faculty who are used to taking charge may not work. You will need to ponder what will. Suppose you learn that you have to design a workshop for 15 junior lecturers. You decide to involve them in a group discussion, but you know that you will need to reassure them when you learn that three of their department heads will be present as well. They may be more reluctant to talk. Or you may have to figure out how to structure what you say to keep 100 people at a conference, including 75 academics and 25 businesspeople, interested in a talk on organizational culture that is scheduled for 2:30 on Monday of Thanksgiving week. Finding creative solutions to these challenges is part of the pain and joy of speaking, just as it is in teaching.

You can see that it is next to impossible to give the same talk twice, much as we'd like to, because as you gather the information based on the answers to the five Ws—plus the additional five questions of how, why me, how long, who else, and how many—you are making decisions about what to say, how to say it, or what not to say. In planning meetings for a conference, you may assert your recommendations based on your awareness of possible human conflicts or venue limitations. You may be negotiating for 5 or 10 minutes more or less or for a room that is bigger or smaller, or perhaps you are recommending that the talk should be given to two groups rather than to one because of your conviction that the message can be coded and received more accurately by doing it that way. By probing in advance, you will be better able to decide what you may want the participants to do and what you will do as well. A few minutes spent asking a series of key questions, and possibly making recommendations for change based on the answers, will enable you to move armed with invaluable information to the next phase of the process, the preparation of your speech.

Therefore, before collecting your notes or thoughts, get ready by asking the following series of questions:

- Why me?
- How long?
- Who else?
- How many?
- Where?
- When?
- Who?
- What?
- Why?
- How?

Once you have the answers, then it is time to create your talk.

# 6 | Preparing Formal Presentations

*To communicate, put your thoughts in order; give them a
purpose; use them to persuade, to instruct, to discover, to seduce.*
— William Safire, columnist, *New York Times*

*A speech is a solemn responsibility. The man who makes a bad
30-minute speech to 200 people wastes only a half hour of his
time. But he wastes 100 hours of the audience's time—more than
4 days—which should be a hanging offense.*
— Jenkin Lloyd Jones, American writer

Let's now look at the process of preparing formal presentations, first in terms of selecting data to support your message
or purpose; second, in terms of how best to organize your
thoughts; and third, in terms of some of the actual word choices
that you make, noting words or phrases to include or exclude.

Once you have asked and answered the questions listed in
Chapter 5, it is time to start collecting the data that you will
need for the talk itself. Your objective is to make your point or
points clearly, accurately, and convincingly. Gathering the
data may require interviewing, reading and/or reflecting, and
analyzing. As with most research, you will accumulate more
information than you need. Too often, speakers, having gathered the data, include all of it or too much of it in the finished
talk. In speech making, less is often more. Overloading the
audience with too much information, particularly if it is theoretical or abstract, is death to the audience and to the speaker.

Instead, with the subject and purpose of the talk clear in your own mind, sift through all the data you have, eliminating what may be tangential or charming but that is irrelevant to the point or points you want to make. Beware that you don't get caught in the trap of preparing a talk that is in fact a journal article. Your audience cannot stop to reflect or reread.

## Selecting Data to Support Your Message

For your talk, select only the information that establishes the context and supports your arguments for the position you are espousing. Suppose you have material on the introduction of a new curriculum in your department—the subject of your talk. In your research, you have found data on the reactions of students at other colleges and universities. Be ruthless and save the inappropriate data about student reactions for another talk if it is not relevant to this one. Don't forget that preparing a talk, like writing a report, is a time management issue. You need time to refine it. Remember the old line: "Forgive the long letter, I didn't have time to write you a short one." The same is true of talks; you need time to prepare a good one.

How you initially organize that mass of data is up to you. You probably have developed an efficient organizing technique at this point in your career. Some people like to make lists of bullet points or to jot down random thoughts. Others prefer to outline their thoughts. Still others write headings and group relevant ideas under each one. Putting your thoughts together for a talk is no different from organizing your ideas for a research report or an article, so select whatever method works well for you. What is important is that you go through the process and take time to create a preliminary structure or outline.

Keep in mind the fact that you are constrained when you talk by the necessity of relying on your verbal clarity. When an audience can only listen, there is no next paragraph or appendix for the reader to read, or to reread, for that matter. When they read your article, they can go back; when you give a talk, they cannot. You are also constrained by the amount of time you have to discuss your subject. Therefore, you have to be sure to select only that information that keeps you on target and that can be absorbed. Although your research has findings, conclusions, and recommendations, the reality is that you may only have the time to adequately and intelligently discuss one or two recommendations. Say so at the outset. In other words, just as research has "limitations," so does a good talk. You tell the audience precisely what the parameters are and thereby let them know what they should not expect to hear. In that way, you narrow their focus and expectations to only those points that you plan to talk about. They will not anticipate more than that.

For example, suppose you are going to talk about a tutorial system. You may indicate that you are speaking only about the one for undergraduates, not the one for the graduate students, or you may indicate that you are speaking only about the system that has been in place for the past 3 years, not the older one.

In addition, by having asked all the preparatory questions, you should have a good idea about the audience's level of knowledge about your topic as well as their frames of reference. Because of that, you can decide what terms or concepts, if any, need to be defined or explained or how much of the context must be clarified for them. Suppose you are asked to discuss the results of a recent survey. If your earlier probing establishes that your audience already knows about the survey, you will not need to devote time explaining the intent, rationale, or methodology. Instead, you will be able to devote your 20 to 25 minutes to discussing only the findings of the survey. If, however, you learn that most of the audience is not aware that a survey was undertaken, a few minutes will have to be spent on bringing them into the picture. In the same way a filmmaker may begin a movie with an aerial shot of Chicago and then zoom in on the street, then on the house, and then on the room in which the action takes place.

Of course, it is always more difficult to gauge what is essential to include in a talk when you have a diverse group coming from different departments, majors, or backgrounds. What may be old hat to the business faculty may be new to the members of the classics department or vice versa. Their perspectives on issues may be equally varied, so you must seek a balance that neither ignores one group nor demeans another. Sometimes the best way to do that is simply to acknowledge orally the degree of diversity. This could be stated as simply as, "Although most of you are familiar with _____ , let me clarify _____ ."

By now you know precisely what the subject is and why you are talking about it. You are collecting the essential and eliminating the nonessential data on the topic. As you are doing so, you are also trying to anticipate questions or arguments about the subject matter. Salespeople sometimes call this process "overcoming objections." To prepare, you need to think through the topic and examine it from the audience's perspective. You then build into your speech their anticipated arguments and objections. You might say, for example, "Some of you may be wondering why we need to undertake a survey at all, when the previous _____ ," and then proceed to explain why. Another approach is to indicate that you are aware that "Some people may have questions, which I will answer later." Once again, your audience must stay foremost in your thoughts.

## How Best to Organize: The Structure

So far, you have asked those key questions. You have gathered, included, excluded, added, and deleted certain ideas. You are anticipating objections. You have identified those points that are essential to making your position clear. It is time now to refine the initial structure for the speech and to organize the material within it. Just as the questions that you asked in preparation came as no surprise to you, this next step in the process should not surprise you either. Quite simply, the talk needs a beginning, a middle, and an end. It is important to know what you want to accomplish in each of the three sections.

Briefly, the first section, the beginning of the talk, is designed to get the audience's full attention, to focus their thoughts on you and on what you are saying. It is the part of the speech in which you state the objectives of the talk, sometimes mentioning its length and the approach that you plan to use. "During the next 20 minutes," you might say, "we will review point by point the _____ ." It is here that you might also include the limitations, that is, what you are *not* going to talk about. "While our research addresses _____ , I will be talking only about _____ , not _____ ."

The middle section of the talk develops your points and is the section in which you explain or elaborate on each of your arguments or ideas. It is the heart of the speech or lecture and is the place where you present the data that you have accumulated and organized.

The end of the talk restates your original objective and may be the time when you ask the audience to take some kind of action based on what you have said. For example, suppose that you state in the beginning that the objective of the talk is to present the conclusions from your research. Then, in the closing when you restate your objective, you tell the audience what you want them to do: consider the findings, read the paper, alter their thinking, encourage their students, lobby for funding, disregard a previous theorist's work, continue the research, or hire you as a consultant. You are stating exactly what it is that you want from them. Thus, as they leave the room or you leave the dais, your message is with them.

Those are the three sections of a talk. Now let's examine each one in more depth.

## The Beginning

Even though you typically will write your opening last, let's talk about it here. Part of the intent of your talk's beginning is to be motivational and to have people focus on you and your words, so let's look at some of the methods by which you can coax people to take their minds off of their other responsibilities and to listen to you.

The most straightforward approach is to state your objective: "Smoking is considered a health hazard, and today we will review the latest medical findings from Ottawa." There are other techniques for opening sentences that you may want to use. For example, you may want to begin with a quotation: "Herman Melville began *Moby Dick* with 'Call me Ishmael.' " Or you may want to tell a story or an anecdote: "A few years ago a friend of mine told the story of a rich woman and a beggar." Or "The last time I spoke in Gainesville . . ." Or "There is a wonderful story of the tourist and the camel." If you are a good joke teller, you may want to try humor as an approach. Jokes, though, can be worrisome, because no matter how witty you are, the audience may not be amused. If you are not feeling confident to begin with, and if the joke falls flat and your audience does not laugh, then the initial setback may only make you feel more uncomfortable. If you are a born story teller, however, use the gift.

Another way to begin a talk is with a question: "When was the last time you wrote a letter?" or "How many of you understand cyberspace?" Yet another technique is the use of a statistic or a shocking fact. A now famous opener was used by a professor of medicine who gazed out at his first-year students and asked them to look first to their right and then to their left, "because," he said, "only one out of the three of you will be sitting here on the first day of term next year." You can be certain that he had their attention!

Some people can use dramatic approaches, make dramatic entrances, make strange noises, throw things, wear shocking clothing, or burst balloons, but that kind of approach does not work for everyone. The downside risk of that kind of theatricality is that the audience may remember the balloons but not the talk that followed their bursting. A colleague of mine tells a story of a keynote speaker who rode into the room on a donkey. I asked what the speech was about. He had no idea.

In other words, you have a variety of options from which to choose. The choices for opening lines are limited only by your imagination, the nature of the event, and the nature of the audience, so you may want to experiment with different styles to determine what works for you. Once again, time of day, other speakers' remarks, or current events may spark an idea. That is why you usually prepare the first few sentences last.

## The Middle

As you structure the middle of your talk, it is vital to remember what we said earlier about inattentiveness being a barrier to effective communication. As you design your presentation, repeat key words, ideas, or phrases. Virtually every TV commercial illustrates this, because new ideas are fragile, like new behaviors, such as trying not to say "um" or excessively using your hands for emphasis. Until the idea is ingrained, the listener may forget it, so repeat your key points. Remember how you were taught vocabulary as a youngster or when you were learning another language? Repetition. Repetition. Repetition. Bear that experience in mind when you prepare your talk.

Make sure you "structure" your talk, creating some sort of logical sequence or progression. Even if you are using visuals in an oral presentation, the audience is dependent on listening to your words, so spend time finding mechanisms to sequence the middle of your talk. Let's look at some of them.

*Numbering.* As we said, the heart of your presentation is the middle. It is in this section of your speech that you develop the arguments, positions, or explanations that you indicated you were going to talk about. Suppose, as we said earlier, that you have been asked to talk about the conclusions based on your research. You tell the audience at the outset that there are 10 conclusions and that you intend to discuss 5 of them. Therefore, in the body of the talk, you develop or explain each one of the 5. The audience now expects you to do this. In their notes, they may have already written the numbers 1 through 5. You say, "the first . . ." and later "the second . . ." as you go.

In other talks you may not have a list but, instead, have a process to describe, the stages or phases of a plan to explain, or a new model to clarify. In the middle of the talk, you explain, clarify, or justify each of the five steps in a logical sequence. You may be giving a talk in which you are arguing both for and against something. In this instance, you may organize the middle by discussing all five positives first and then the five negatives, or one pro and then one con, then the next pro and the next con, and so on. Regardless of your approach, you must create a logical sequence. Again you say, "There are five reasons for and five reasons against. The first . . ." It might seem obvious, but think of the talks you've heard when you lost the thread or the meaning because the speaker didn't help you stay on track.

Numbering is always useful. It helps the audience take notes, to say nothing of the fact that you have fingers on your hands that might be useful. Be sure, though, that if you decide to use numbers, do so consistently. If you say that you have five points, do not mention number one, number two, number four, and number five and forget to say the number three. Invariably the members of the audience will check with their neighbors to find out what happened to number three. They will be talking to each other, not listening to you.

*Order of Importance.* Suppose you have five arguments to support your recommendations. You now need to decide in what order to put the five—which is number one and which are numbers two, three, four, and five? Make a decision about the sequence. You may want to let the audience know what that decision is, but do not just let the order happen because it was simply the order in which you collected the data. Decide if you want the most important reason first. Do you want it last? That decision affects where the least important reason goes, first or last. Which arguments do you want in the middle of your list? In what order? Why?

*Chronology.* Maybe the subject of your talk is historical and, therefore, has to do with what was, what is, and what will be. Then, a natural sequence for your presentation might be chronological order—past to present to future. Or it might be more effective to work in the opposite direction, future to past. Again, keep in mind that the audience is being asked to recall information primarily by hearing. In the absence of a script, numbered lists and chronologically ordered information will assist your audience in following your train of thought as well as helping them to retain it.

*Theory to Practice or Theory to Application.* Numbering is not always possible or appropriate. Suppose, for example, that you want to explain a theoretical construct. Theory is abstract, difficult to visualize, and intangible, so it is essential that you give the audience an example of the theory at work or an example of its application. Recall Maslow's hierarchy of needs. It is invariably pictured as a pyramid, a device that helps you to visualize the concept. The top of the pyramid is usually labeled "self-actualization." But what does that mean? You cannot hold or touch self-actualization. So, if you think back to the first time you encountered that particular pyramid, the author or the instructor probably gave you examples of what self-actualization means to real people or asked what it meant to you in order to clarify that idea. In other words, it is important to describe a theoretical concept with a concrete image, an analogy, or an example. You can talk about an internal combustion engine, or you can see one. You can discuss strategic planning, but it helps to visualize it. You can talk about information technology, but you need to give the audience something to hold on to in the form of an image, application, example, or analogy. Imagine trying to persuade students to visit your campus without showing them any pictures of the library, the chemistry labs, or the student lounge.

*Spatial.* Suppose your talk is not about theory, but about architecture, art, or geography; the layout of an office building; a painting; or a new geological find. Perhaps you may decide to organize your talk spatially, moving from the description of the left side of the building to the right, from the top to the bottom, or from the bottom to the top. You may talk about the painting from the center out. Again, what you are doing is planning your talk to enable the audience to follow your verbal logic. What if the subject is geographical? Do you want it organized in terms of east to west or north to south or the reverse?

*Mnemonics.* Another mechanism for creating internal structure is by using memory aids—mnemonics. As you organize your thoughts, you will discover that certain key words or ideas stand out. When you write them down, note the first letter of each word. Can you make a word from those letters that will help the audience remember your key ideas? For example, "Today we are examining a DREAM." You then explain that the letter D stands for development, R for research, and so on. Each letter represents one of the points that you want to make. The objective of using the mnemonic is to help the listener remember the points. As always there is a caveat: Be careful that your mnemonic is not too long, as is, for example, ENVIRONMENT: E = energy, N = nature, V = vegetation, and so on. The audience may remember only the mnemonic and not what it stands for, just as my colleague remembered the donkey and not the point of his boss' talk.

These are some methods, but if none of these approaches fits the subject of the talk, then you need to look for other methods of organizing the data. Find one. Could the talk be organized in terms of threats and opportunities or in terms of similarities and differences? Could you raise several questions and then answer each one in turn? Might you talk of the macro issues and then the micro? Could the organization be in terms of themes?

To recap: By now you have finished preparing the middle of your talk and have determined what you are going to say, why you are going to say it, what data you plan to use to substantiate your arguments, and how you are organizing it. In so doing, you may eliminate material because it may have been merely tangential or essential. Therefore, check the opening, which is designed to motivate the audience to listen and to establish the objectives. You may need to adjust it to reflect your internal modifications. The same is true of the closing.

## The Closing

As we said earlier, the closing restates your objective and may recommend a next step. People remember the beginning and end of a talk better than they remember the middle, so you need to find an effective way to grab their attention at the outset and then to underline the importance of what you have told them and what you want from them. Those aspects are too important to be left to chance.

Let's look at closings. In addition to signaling that the end of the talk is near by saying "in conclusion" or "finally," you have exactly the same choices for ending a talk as you do for beginning one. For example, suppose you chose to start the talk with the Herman Melville quotation; you might then want to end it with the same one or another by Melville, or one by another American author. Suppose you decided to begin by asking a question; you might consider ending with the answer to the opening question, by restating the original one, or by asking yet another one. Start with a story, end with a story. Start with a statistic, close with one. What is important to realize is that, once again, you have to make a decision in advance. By the way, if you choose to close with "in conclusion" or "in summary," be careful to conclude only once, not as some speakers insist on doing—over and over again.

This, then, is the basic organization of the talk. So far, so good: a beginning with a solid appropriate attention-getting device, a statement of the objectives, and explanation of the limitations, followed by a middle that is logically sequenced and a closing that restates your objectives—the what and why you were talking about the subject. What you have done is outline the talk. It is a strong skeleton. Now you have to flesh it out with words and examples. How do you do that?

## Selecting Your Words

It is impossible here to review every word or phrase you might use in a talk; however, let's examine some of the frequently selected words and phrases that you should consider including or eliminating in the same way that there are certain gestures or other movements that enhance or detract from your presentation.

### Be Specific

First of all, be specific whenever possible. When you choose words like "huge," "tremendous," "great," "wonderful," "vast," "costly," and "enormous," the audience has no frame of reference. Is it as "vast" as Central Park or the Mojave Desert? In other words, my idea of "huge" may be different from yours. What is "costly" to me may be a pittance to you. Is a "stack" of mail a foot deep or an inch deep? Therefore, use specifics: 15%, $4, next Tuesday, 2 feet, Kohlberg's findings. The more specific you can be, the less your audience will suffer from confusion. Look at all the quiz shows and board games like "Trivial Pursuit" that proliferate because of our ability to retain specifics. How did James Bond take his martini: "Shaken, not _____"? Think about what you remember from talks you've sat through; frequently, it is a fact or an example.

## Use Analogies and Verbal Images

Another useful tool is to make analogies or give verbal images that bring your subject to life. Is the department budget equivalent to the national debt? Were the hailstones the size of golf balls? Was the office so crowded it looked like Sears on a Saturday morning? Was it so hot that you could fry eggs on the sidewalk? In other words, whenever possible provide verbal images, specifics, or analogies to which the audience can relate.

## Be Careful Not to Demean

Let's eliminate a group of words quickly. Those are words or phrases that may be inappropriate, clever, or sarcastic and remarks that are demeaning, insulting, or stereotyping and that touch on such items as sex, job, age, religion, ethnic background, politics, and disability. You know the list, but, in preparing your talk, you need to double check that you have not slipped something into your talk by mistake. It is easy to offend, and, when you do, you risk alienating someone who may be a member of a particular group or related to someone who is, or who may have strong feelings on the subject.

When you refer to graduate assistants as "girls," deans as "hes," or people over 50 as "sedentary," you risk offending. Let the audience make the snide comment about a recent political faux pas in some country; don't do it for them. An inappropriate reference may cost you some members of the audience. They may focus on the remark, think about it, and either lose the flow of the talk or, worse yet, resent you because you have enunciated values that are incompatible with their own. It is an expensive error. Let's be clear that what is being referred to is your choice of examples or asides. The subject matter itself may be difficult for some people to accept. Be careful of inadvertent insults or inside jokes.

## Watch for Mistakes

Also, be mindful when you select your supporting data that you do not say something that is wrong, inaccurate, illegal, or unethical. Suppose, for example, that you cite references to events that you think occurred in 1989 but actually occurred in 1991. There will surely be someone in the audience who is aware of the error and will see a crack in your credibility. You will have a difficult time regaining it. If one statistic is wrong, they'll question whether there are others. A guest lecturer in Dublin recently referred to his pleasure at being in the British Isles. He didn't know his facts, and the audience groaned. His credibility waned.

## Eliminate Pet Phrases

You will probably be ready to run through your talk now, so as you do, another recommendation about word choice involves less dangerous ground than offending or making factual mistakes. Some words are just annoying or distracting. They are single words, analogies, or phrases such as "as you know," "at this stage," "as such," "OK," "well," or "right." There is nothing wrong with any one of them, but you would be amazed at how many times a pet phrase is sprinkled throughout a talk without the speaker realizing it. These words and phrases constitute a problem only when they are used with such frequency that the audience notices them and begins to count. For example, if you say "OK" at the end of every sentence or every time you change a transparency, you may find that the audience is beginning to keep track of those "OKs" on the corners of their notes.

It is important to notice if you do have the tendency to repeat certain expressions, because you risk the audience focusing on the "you know" rather than the rest of your talk. Catch yourself if you are in the habit of starting a sentence with "Well" or "Right." Think of the wasted effort. All that time you have devoted to developing a clear message, good structure, and the right opening words only to ruin things by sprinkling your presentation with "well." You cure yourself of this the same way that you cure yourself of other habits: Catch yourself doing it and then gradually decrease its use.

## Avoid Unnecessary Apologies

Another caveat about phrases: Watch out for the self-deprecating ones such as "I hope that I did not bore you," "I am *just* going to talk about _____," "I am only going to take a few minutes," "Thanks for listening," or, when you close, "Well, that's it!" Sometimes the phrases suggest that you didn't prepare: "I hope the technology works. Which is the on/off button?" All that work, planning, organizing, structuring, and looking for examples and analogies—what are you apologizing for? You may think the phrases or words will endear you to the audience. In fact, they can have a negative effect. Before there is any misunderstanding, let me clarify. The phrase "I am just going to talk about _____" is very different from telling a story about yourself, about a mistake you made, or the weight that you have gained over the vacation. Revealing a foible can be charming and may help establish rapport. However, your audience expects a professional, so you should not apologize or undermine your work. If you have taken the responsibility for the talk, be proud and own the moment. Make no apologies when none are called for.

## Avoid "I'm Going to Talk About . . ."

There is another particular sentence that you should avoid using. Many presentations begin with "Today I am going to talk about aid to developing nations." Consider eliminating that phrase and instead plunging right into the talk. For example, instead of "I am going to talk about the importance of giving aid to developing nations," try "Increasing our aid to developing nations is important." It is more direct. While we are at it, think about whether it is "I" or "We." "I" separates; "We" joins. So, if you believe that your message will be received better with "We," by all means use it. It suggests that you and your audience are engaged in the enterprise together.

## Come to the End Once

We've all heard many speakers say "finally," then keep on talking and add "and, my last point is _____ ," then keep on talking and add, "so, in summary _____" and then keep on talking and add, "therefore, to conclude _____ ." "Finally" or "In conclusion" should be said only once—when your talk is almost over. You are signaling to the audience that you are finished. They expect it to be over. Be careful to end your talk once.

## Pause Before "Thank You"

Finally, there is "Thank you." The objective of the final sentence in your talk is to reinforce your main points or underline your message, so take care not to let your "thank you" slide into the final words. Say your final sentence and then pause. Think about what usually happens at the end: The speaker receives a well-earned round of applause or is thanked by some key person on behalf of the others present. The audience says "thank you" for the talk with their applause. The speaker then thanks *them* for their expression of gratitude, be it applause or kind words. "Why all the fuss about such a simple point?" you ask. It is a pity to hear a well-thought-out final idea blurred or lost by closing amenities. Say what you have to say, pause or stop, and then acknowledge the applause. You will have earned it!

In summary, having asked your questions, you assemble the data, bearing your purpose and audience in mind. You then organize your talk into three sections, carefully sequencing the middle so as to aid retention. Both the beginning and the end state your message and ensure that attention is being paid. Once you have drafted your talk, you look for ways to bring in analogies and specifics, ensuring that they are accurate and not offensive. Having drafted the talk, you will begin practicing, so take care not to include extraneous words and remarks that, like inappropriate body language, detract from your key ideas.

# 7 | Preparing Other Presentations

*What we have here is a failure to communicate.*
—from the movie *Cool Hand Luke*

In the course of our careers, we are not always spending our time preparing to deliver scholarly papers or 45-minute talks on aspects of our degree programs to visiting lecturers or to members of associations. In fact, much of our time is spent giving a variety of other kinds of presentations. These may range from speaking for 5 to 10 minutes at a faculty, department, or committee meeting to giving a commencement address that we hope will be inspirational to participating at a luncheon meeting, brown-bag seminar, or round-table discussion. Other talks might be at workshops in the form of an introduction or a thank you to guest speaker. At some point, you have undoubtedly found yourself moderating a panel, being on an interview board, interviewing for a position yourself, or defending a thesis. Whether you are speaking for a minute, for 5 minutes, or for more, or whether you are answering the questions or posing them, you are on the hot seat. You are the center of attention for those moments, so you can view each and every one of these events as a presentation.

Therefore, what are the differences, if any, between these types of presentations and the 45-minute formal talk? What can you do to prepare for them? How can you become more effective and ensure that you don't have a "failure to communicate" in these varied situations?

*The Formality Changes.* If you analyze the nature of each of these diverse events, you will realize that there is very little difference between these various formats and formal presentations. You speak and someone else listens; however, the degree of formality may change. Addressing the combined masses of parents, faculty, and students in a ballroom or amphitheater is far more formal than sitting in a seminar room, debating with 10 colleagues an issue of shared interest. That altered formality will manifest itself in your choice of clothing, words, and posture.

*The Interaction Varies.* Along with the formality, the degree of interaction changes as well. Standing behind a lectern, presenting your research findings to a group of 700, is quite different from sitting in a straight-backed chair as a candidate for a position and being on the receiving end of an interview panel's questions. The formal presentation is primarily a planned, one-way communication experience with a few minutes devoted to handling questions, whereas the interview may be more of a ping-pong or tennis match with questions and answers moving back and forth across the table or around the room. Interestingly, some interview boards are combining the two approaches by requesting candidates to prepare 5- to 10-minute presentations in advance. The topics may be about the candidate's strengths or about what he or she can bring to the position.

*The Proximity Alters.* In a formal talk, you may find that you are 15 to 20 feet away from your audience. When you sit across an interview table or elbow to elbow over lunch, you are close to each other. The nuances of your nonverbal behavior, the modulation of your voice, and your choice of clothing are noticed because of the degree of intimacy. In interview situations, notice how the trembling hand, the darting eye, and the idiosyncratic nervous gesture is now magnified and interpreted far more than from the front row of a lecture theater.

*The Control Shifts.* Therefore, in addition to the degree of formality changing and the degree of interaction altering, your ability to control all the elements of the event alters as well. In a 45-minute talk, you write the speech, prepare the visuals, deliver the talk uninterrupted, and take a question or two, deciding when you have time for one or no more. On the other hand, around a seminar table, in a meeting of 12 colleagues on a committee or at an interview, you are interacting with diverse personalities, with differing styles and agendas. You have less control, and you have to be more spontaneous. What can you do? Prepare.

*What You Do to Prepare.* You do exactly what you would do if you were preparing to give a lecture. You would ask yourself or the organizer exactly the same set of questions in order to prepare for a less formal or more intimate event. You ask how, what, where, why, how, and who else? How many and why me? Thus, you anticipate the kinds of issues or questions that you are going to be faced with. Some of the questions may be predictable, as they might be with an interview panel, that is, why are you applying, long-term goals, and so on. Regardless of the situation, you should ask, Who is going to be there? What perspectives might members of the audience have on the subject at hand? How many will there be: 3, 5, 15? How much time will you have? One hour, one and a half? How will the room be organized? Will you be seated around a lunch table, in chairs in classroom style, or in a V-shape? Will sandwiches or snacks be served? What's the purpose of the event, and what message are you trying to get across? Your message may be that you have more to offer the interview panel than anyone else or that you know your subject or that you would welcome new ideas. Bearing in mind that formality, proximity, control, and interaction change, your preparation is identical with that for a formal talk. You are asking yourself, "What am I trying to accomplish and why?"

Inasmuch as there will undoubtedly be questions and answers, one of the best methods of preparing is to ask a friend or colleague to put you through your paces by way of a mock interview or to ask you some challenging questions that the particular group might ask. How do you know what they'll ask? One useful method is to turn the situation around and view the topic from the perspectives of the questioners.

## Listen

What does alter considerably is your need to use your listening ability. In an interactive environment, as you well know from teaching, it is vital that the participants are actively listening or concentrating on what is being said or asked. Although we'll be looking at handling questions in Chapter 10, it is critical to underline here that you as a player in such a situation should be concentrating and listening carefully to all the questions being asked or the comments made, even those not directed to you. If they are for you, probe them, if the intent is not clear, by seeking amplification. You may want to restate or paraphrase the question or comment to be sure that you have understood the point as it was intended. If you are a member of a panel, you may very well want to have a pen and paper with you, because you cannot always guarantee that you will be the next to speak. You may want to return to a point made earlier if it is appropriate and if you think it is warranted in order to move the discussion along. The same need to listen is equally true if you are thanking a guest speaker at the end of the talk. It is often a gracious and effective technique to close an event by referring to some of the comments or challenges made by the speaker. That can be accomplished only if you listen carefully and jot some notes as you go. Certainly you can prepare the skeleton in advance, but you can flesh it out only during the talk.

## Pay Attention to Detail

Ask preparatory questions, listen, and remember that you are physically closer to your audience. As we mentioned earlier, when you are sitting around a room or presenting to a small group or taking question after question as you would in an interview, what you do with your face, your body, your hands, and your choice of clothing are as important as when you stand on the podium in a lecture theater. There is greater intimacy, and, therefore, detail will be more apparent. Although you can appear to be looking at everyone by moving your head from right to left from behind a dais, when you are settled around a table with an interview board or with prospective clients for a consulting opportunity, then you should be making eye contact with everyone present, regardless of who asks you what question. Although you may be sitting, you should appear eager and attentive by sitting up and forward. Your face should exude warmth and enthusiasm, be it in defense of your thesis or in eagerness for the position for which you are applying. Be wary of inadvertently rolling your eyes or looking exasperated or disgusted. Pay attention to the condition of your clothing, your fingernails, and the notes you jot down. In these arenas, nothing will be missed.

## Be Polite

You will gain support around a table if you refer to your colleagues by name, for example, "As John said earlier . . ." or "Dr. Brown's comments are . . ." Be wary of inside jokes or secrets. Although individuals may welcome being identified by name, they may resent being kept in the dark about some story. Tell them or don't, but don't hint and grin, for example, "You remember last time, John?" It's rude.

## If You Are in Charge, Be the Host

Preparation, warmth, and control are particularly important if you are moderating a panel or introducing a speaker. Frequently, in those situations, you are charged by a conference or meeting organizer to keep the session on time and on track.

Therefore, you should be sure that you have the opportunity in advance in person, by phone, by fax, or by e-mail to determine exactly what the speaker wants you to say by way of introduction. How often have you been the speaker and heard your name being mispronounced, a wrong degree awarded, a college renamed, or your talk retitled simply because you met each other for 30 seconds on the way into the lobby or at the podium? Just as you may wish to be introduced in a particular manner, so do your colleagues.

Controlling the event is difficult. Guest speakers have been known to become enchanted with the sound of their own voices or to turn the talk toward a particular "hobby horse" that they adore. You are the clock watcher, and this is the time when you have to do your job and be the gracious, observant host that you have been asked to be. There will be times when you will have one eye on the clock and two ears on the panelist. You may have to cut the speaker off or the questions. You need to be empathetic and have a few prepared phrases: "Unfortunately, our time is limited and we can take only two more questions," or "Perhaps during the break, . . ." The same skills are needed if you are the moderator and one panelist is silent. It is incumbent on you as the chair to involve all the panelists or committee members, with a specific question or by calling for a reaction to a previous speaker: "Do you agree?" or "What has your experience been?" or "John, would you tell the story?" You are the host and conductor at the same time. You want the panelists to feel at ease and yet you have to ensure that a dialogue among all of them has been created.

Seminars, interviews, and workshops may appear to be quite different from delivering papers because of the following:

- The formality changes
- The interaction varies
- The proximity alters
- The control shifts

You have to prepare in the same way as you would for a formal talk. In addition, you should:

- Listen
- Pay attention to detail
- Be polite
- Be the host, if you are in charge

# 8 | Using Notes

*William Graham spoke without a note, and almost without a point.*

—Winston Churchill

$N$ow that your talk has been thought through and drafted, it is time to make yet another decision about your notes. This chapter addresses the importance of notes and how to use cards as prompts. We will not be discussing electronic options, such as teleprompters.

In essence, you now have to decide whether to write the talk out in longhand, type it, print it, and then read it word for word, or whether to jot notes on paper or on cards and then speak extemporaneously. Some speakers may decide to memorize the whole talk. Having already read about my fiasco of years ago, when I went blank, you know that I would always advise against relying strictly on memory. The downside risk is enormous. If anything goes wrong that causes you to lose your train of thought or that causes you to become unduly anxious, then the worst can happen and your doubts will be realized—you may forget it all. If you ask other speakers, you will discover that memory lapse does happen to speakers at one time or another. It is possible to look at the audience and to panic or to lose your train of thought because of a technical hitch, untoward interruption, or unexpected disturbance. It does not happen often, but it can, so unless you have a masochistic need to experience that disaster or discomfort, use notes of some type. Having notes humanizes you in the eyes of the audience and thus makes you more credible.

## Reading Versus Using Notes

Before looking more closely at what you write for notes, let's return to the notion of reading the speech. You often see that approach at professional conferences where presenters "deliver a paper." Reading papers is not about establishing rapport; it is hard to establish any eye contact, to weigh reactions, and to respond by altering pace, pitch, volume, or content. Try reading this page as if there were an audience present. Notice that if you even think of looking up from the page to look out at the audience, it is easy to lose your place, and then your poise.

Reading a paper also makes you more dependent on a lectern, because you need to put the pages on something. If you hold them in your hands, the pages are awkward, particularly as you read near the bottom or have to turn them. Paper is noisy, and, if you're using a microphone, everyone in the room may hear the sheets crackling. If, however, you do decide to read, be sure to use good quality paper and not pages torn from a legal pad. You probably have seen that, and it is not a pretty sight. It may give the audience the impression that you wrote the talk on the way over to the meeting. The audience wants to know that you have invested time in them. Also use large type that you can easily read and rehearse and rehearse, so you know the text well enough to be able to lift your head from the pages.

Some presenters use their overheads or slides as prompts or notes. We will be discussing visuals in the next chapter, but using slides as prompts raises some more questions. You should ask yourself whether the visuals were designed for your use or for the audience. Slides that are the speaker's notes usually have too much written on them. Did you have to design too many of them, because they were your notes? Or are you speaking extemporaneously until you turn on your first overhead or slide? In other words, unless you strike some kind of balance, you could leave yourself vulnerable at the outset without any prompts, or have too many slides or cluttered, poorly executed ones, because they are designed for you, not for the audience.

You have detected my bias: It is better to use notes than to read and to use cards for your notes rather than turning your visuals into notes. Why cards? Paper, as noted previously, is awkward and noisy; 3×5 or 4×6 cards are not. They fit in your hand; they also fit in a pocket, which means you can carry them and practice conveniently. For those of you who don't know what to do with your hands, cards give you something to hold, and unless you shuffle them, they will not make any noise. They also free you from the lectern and allow you to move.

## Using Note Cards

What do you put on the cards? First of all, you should write on only one side of the card and then number them in sequence, just in case they become disordered. Write in letters large enough to enable you to see them if you were holding them at arm's length. On each card you might write one of your key ideas, justifications, or rationales. After the key idea should be a word or a few words to remind you of the examples that you plan to use to bring that idea to life.

If you have a new idea later, all you have to do is add a card or destroy one. You do not have to retype the whole speech or squeeze in your ideas on the margin of the paper. In fact, you may want one card on which the opening is completely written out. That is extra insurance at the beginning when you are most anxious and might want the additional support. In addition to your cards with the key ideas, you may also want to reproduce your slides or acetates onto your cards. In that way you will not have to turn your back to the audience when you show them. The words on the slide will be in your hand as well as reproduced on the screen.

## Practicing With Notes

Now you need to begin to practice your talk using your note cards. As you do, you will notice that there are a number of other advantages to using note cards beside the fact that they are noiseless and fit in your pocket. During your talk, they allow you to be more mobile. Remember that sheets of paper keep you near the lectern, and that is not always desirable. A static figure is less interesting than one that moves. The only support the cards need is from your hands, so you are freer to walk around the room. In addition, as was mentioned earlier, the cards give you something to do with your hands, thus taking care of one or two of those extra appendages that appeared when you walked to the front of the room. In addition, you can hold your hands in such a way that a quick glance down at your notes is all that is needed for you to continue. Thus, you break your eye contact with the audience only briefly.

If you have never used cards before, it takes time to adjust to them. Two points, as you practice: First, if you know that you have the habit of holding your hands together as you speak, do not hold onto the cards in the same way. One hand should hold the pack, the other should hold the card that you are referring to. When you are finished with it, move it to the bottom of the pack. The second recommendation is to hold them all with pride. Try not to fidget with the cards, to turn them around, or to tap with them. If you do, then the notes themselves become a distraction. When you have referred to your note, do not throw the finished card on the nearest table, as if you cannot wait to be rid of it. Remember, they represent hours of preparation reduced to a pack of 3×5 cards.

As you become more used to working with notes you may find them reassuring to have as well. With your key words or phrases written down, you eliminate the fear of blanking out and you know what you are going to say. In addition, notes also serve to bring you back on track, if you are distracted by someone or something in the audience. Perhaps someone asked a question in midstream or you thought of a good story to tell. Notes serve to remind you where you left off and where you still need to go to get your message across.

Although there are times when you will want to deliver a paper, whenever possible:

- Use notes rather than read word for word.
- Use your visuals to reinforce your message, not as cue cards.
- Use cards rather than sheets of paper for your notes.
- Write key phrases on the cards and be sure that you have numbered each card.
- Practice developing a comfort level with the cards. As you practice, notice how they allow you greater freedom of movement and how they permit you to develop and maintain rapport with your audience.

# 9 | Using Visuals and Handouts

*Visuals act as punctuation points in your presentation. They offer relief to the audience and make the audience's commitment a series of short decisions to stay tuned instead of one long, unattractive obligation.*

—Ed Brenner, photographer and publisher

*A picture may instantly present what a book could set forth only in a hundred pages.*

—Ivan Turgenev

Visuals have been referred to several times before. This chapter is dedicated to them because they warrant more than a passing reference. Visuals are used to assist the audience in retaining and understanding information. When you see and hear about something at the same time, it will stay in your mind longer. For example, you can describe your office verbally to an audience, but by giving them a picture of it and talking about it simultaneously, you give your audience a far better sense of what you want them to see. You can talk about a Busby Berkeley musical, or you can show a photograph or film clip as you speak. The impact is different. That is why you use visuals. They can consist of words, pictures, graphs, charts, props, or handouts. Let's consider them separately, asking questions as we do.

## Do You Need Visuals?

Once your talk is outlined and your key points and supporting examples for each are thought through carefully, it is time to review your speech and determine when a visual would clarify a point or reinforce your words and what kind of visual would accomplish that best. Remember, you do not use graphics just because you think every talk requires them. You use them because they make a difference. Often a presentation is a follow-up to a study or a report, so many speakers use the written report itself as the basis for the talk. Unfortunately, the visuals are often actual copies of pages taken out of the document, either from the appendix or from the findings. The problem is that the visuals look like exactly that—pages from a report, with page numbers and all.

It is important to remember that written documents are different from talks. One difference is that reports can be read over time by an individual in isolation, re-read, read in sections, put down, and picked up again. Because the reader can pore over a table or a chart in a report at leisure, it can be more detailed and have smaller print than one in a talk. An audience does not have that time. In essence, you cannot necessarily use a visual that was designed for another medium. To repeat: You have to decide what the audience needs to see and how you want them to see it. For example, compare Box 9.1, which consists mainly of text, with the list of bullets in Box 9.2. Compare them in terms of accessibility for an audience:

## Assessing Their Learning: Exams

- *Work for instructional congruency.* That's a fancy way of saying that what you emphasize in class, in the readings, and on homework problems should be emphasized on the exams. You put students in an impossible situation if you include one question from material that you spent 3 days on in class but have four questions on a topic you introduced in the final 15 minutes of a period. If you opt for this approach, you do not encourage students to learn what is important but get them focused on trivia and trying to figure you out. Remember the key question from Chapter 3: What do you want students to know and be able to do at the conclusion of the course? Exams should be designed with that kind of learning in mind.

- *Be concerned about the reliability of the exam.* Exams are like bathroom scales—if the scale is out of adjustment, the measurement is inaccurate. If you write a multiple-choice item that is not clear in its intent, students will choose the wrong answer, not because they do not know the material, but because they cannot make sense of the question. A good exam is like a clean window. It is there, but it doesn't get in the way. It gives you a clear, undistorted view of what a student knows and can do.

- *Err on the side of frequency.* More exams are better than too few, particularly for entry-level students and populations considered at risk. Most of those who study entry-level students counsel against one midterm and one final. After that, the advice is less specific and more dependent on your individual situation. There is probably a point at which exams become so frequent that they cannot really be considered exams. However, most faculty err on the side of too few as opposed to too many.

- *Match desired learning with exam type.* Multiple-choice exams are not inherently better or worse than essay exams, take-home tests, or matching questions. Each exam has assets and liabilities. Some achieve some learning objectives better than others. The decision of which ones or which combination to use should be the result of an attempt to match learning goals and question types.

—from Weimer (1993),
*Improving Your Classroom Teaching*, pp. 99-100

**Box 9.1**

---

### Assessing Their Learning: Exams

- Work for instructional congruency
- Be concerned about the reliability of the exam
- Err on the side of frequency
- Match desired learning with exam type

—from Weimer (1993),
*Improving Your Classroom Teaching*

---

Box 9.2

# What Kind of Visuals Are Most Appropriate for the Occasion?

Before examining what a good visual looks like, you should decide what kind of visuals would be appropriate for the occasion. When you do that, you have to factor in the number of people present in the room and the available technology. Do you want to give them a handout to take with them when they leave the room? Do you think that it would be better for them to have some written material before you start? Do you consider that there is no need at all for slides, videos, handouts, or preprinted transparencies, because you feel that writing on a blackboard or whiteboard as you talk is more effective? Will a flip chart do? Would you prefer to use a presentation package? You should make your decisions based on the answers to your earlier questions: the purpose of the talk, the nature of the topic, the size of the room, and the number of people, all of which affect the degree of formality and interaction you want. Certainly videos and slides are more expensive and time consuming to produce than transparencies or images on a computer monitor, whereas creating your own visual clarification or reinforcements as you talk by writing on a whiteboard or flip chart is more immediate and casual. Another inexpensive option is to "preflip," that is, to write on the flip chart in advance of your talk. If you handwrite or use computer software, you should be asking the same questions.

## What Should You
## Consider in the Design?

Let's suppose you have decided that you need a graphic with the title of your talk on it and then one for each of your key points. In addition, you plan to use one or two more for charts or graphs in order to demonstrate a particular trend that supports your argument, a picture of an artifact you are discussing, and a map indicating some demographic data. Let's examine what you should take into consideration when you design these graphics. First of all, any image primarily devoted to words should be kept simple and should have print large enough and dark enough against the background for everyone in the room to see it. You should also have a generous amount of "white space" around the margins and between the points, so that it is easy to read from anywhere in the room. Avoid complete sentences; instead, use phrases or bullet points. If you use bullet points, be sure that the language of each point is consistent. Look at this:

The purpose of the research was to:

- Determine the _____ .
- Assess the _____ .
- Conclusions about the _____ .

Notice that this speaker begins the first two points with a verb, "determine" and "assess," and the third point with a noun, "conclusions." The third item in the list should, in fact, also be a verb, "conclude." Alternatively, the first two points might be changed to nouns instead, "determination" and "assessment." Then, of course, you would have to change the stem as well: "The purpose of the research was to make _____." This consistency makes it easier for the audience to follow. Also be sure that the points on your graphic are lined up under each other, not two spaces to the left:

- Determine the _____ .
- Assess the _____ .
  - Conclude that _____ .
  - Recommend that _____ .

Such carelessness not only looks sloppy but also distracts your audience. Inconsistent use of upper and lower case is equally annoying:

- Determine the _____ .
- assess the _____ .
- Conclude that _____ .

Do not forget to proofread for typographical errors: "invoolment," "accomodation," and "liason," as well as missing or misplaced apostrophes. A typo signals to the audience that you are inattentive to detail. They may wonder if you did not have time to check on these points and that perhaps some of your other research, remarks, or recommendations are also sloppy. If the audience allows that possibility to enter their minds, you risk the loss of your credibility. If you are under time constraints, it might be wiser not to use visuals than to use any that are less than excellent.

Besides ensuring that you have a good layout, consistent language, and no typos, make sure you have a title or label, particularly with charts and graphs. Too often, speakers spend time creating an excellent visual representation but forget to label it. Bear in mind that people can be distracted by a noise or may come into the talk late. What a pity to have an exquisitely designed pie chart on the screen with percentages carefully indicating each segment, but one that the audience cannot attach meaning to because there is no title. So, label your graphics, especially if you are showing more than one chart or graph.

## What About Using Charts and Graphs?

Suppose you have decided to use a graph in order to demonstrate a trend. It needs to be labeled and titled as well. In fact, you may find that the audience follows your train of thought better if you have one graph showing the basic data, the axis. Then you show the changes by overlaying it with another one that has the new information on it. In that way, the audience can grasp the information bit by bit while you assist them by providing the information in a systematic way.

To highlight a point in your visual, you may want to put an arrow next to a critical bar in the graph or to put a circle around a key intersection. During the presentation, you may use a pointer, remembering never to point it at the audience. You could also verbally tell them where you want them to look: "If you look at the last column on the right, . . ." or "Look at the top of the _____ ." Guide their eyes to the place that you want them to look; otherwise, they will be taking in the information as they choose, not as you wish them to.

Also, look for logical sequences on your visuals, just as you did in the body of the talk. Numbers and years need careful organizing. Stay chronological, if you can: 1990-1991, 1991-1992, not 1993-1994, 1991-1992, 1992-1993. Write north to south, smallest to largest or largest to smallest, and left to right.

Keep the visuals simple, though. If you have "10 Reasons for . . ." all on one visual, the audience may be reading numbers 9 and 10 while you are talking about number 2. You lose the reinforcement potential that way. That is why some speakers use the "revealing technique" by showing only part of a transparency at a time. Not everyone likes that approach. For some it is demeaning or childish. Once again, consider using more visuals, be they slides, acetates, or computer images.

## Do You Allow
## the Audience Time to Read?

If you are using handouts, you might want to tell the audience that you plan to distribute them at the end. However, if you give the audience something to read on a screen or in their hands, remember that they will read it. Therefore, if you do that, here is an opportunity for you to practice your pausing ability by giving them time to read it. In the same way that you have talked them through a graph, map, or chart, you guide them through the words on the visual, by speaking the exact words that are written on the screen. When you speak the words that are on the screen, the audience both hears and sees them. Thus, you are reinforcing your ideas and increasing the odds of the audience's retaining the information that you want them to remember.

## Are You Breaking Eye Contact?

Remember that when you are using visuals, you should not turn to the screen to look at them. Maintain eye contact with the audience. You do not abdicate that responsibility once you include images in your talk. If you are using a screen, stand to one side. Remember, reference to the image is on your cards. Whether you are using individual transparencies or a computer, you can see the picture without turning because it is in front of you on the overhead projector. Therefore, there is no reason for you to turn your back. You can see exactly what your audience is seeing simply by looking at the plate on which the image is lying. With a transparency, you need only turn back quickly to check the screen to ensure that it is not at an angle, that it is right side up, and that it is completely displayed.

If you are using a flip chart or writing on an overhead, do not talk and write at the same time. If you do, you will be projecting your voice back to the board or down to the chart. Say the words and then turn to write them, or write them and then turn back to the audience and say them.

## Have You Anticipated Problems?

Know your equipment. Know your equipment well. In Chapter 11, when we talk about practicing, we will say more about this, but it is important to make the point now as well. One special thought for those of you using presentation packages: Consider having a backup set of transparencies, just in case.

Earlier we mentioned that people will read whatever you distribute to them. If you have decided on using a handout at the beginning of the presentation, know that people will read what you have given them. Build that factor into your plan: "If you look at the second point on the sheet, you will see that it says _____ ." In other words, control what the audience does with what you have distributed. Most people write on handouts, so be sure that you have provided enough "white space" on the paper for them to jot down their notes. Suppose, however, that you want each member of the audience to have a copy of a complex table. Give it to them at the time that they need to refer to it and then specify what aspect you want them to look at: "If you look at the third column, you will notice that it compares _____ ."

To avoid problems—the third person in the fifth row may not have received one, for example—handouts are usually distributed at the end of a talk or are placed at each seat before the audience arrives. If you decide to use replicas or mock-ups, your responsibility is once again to ask yourself, just as you do with handouts or other visuals, what you are using them for and whether the audience will understand them and benefit from their use.

In other words, you once again have a plethora of options to choose from. You need to remember that the purpose of an image is to clarify and/or reinforce your message, so you need to select the best medium for the particular presentation and then to ensure clarity and accuracy.

Therefore, when you have outlined your talk, ask yourself the following questions:

- Do I need visuals?
- What type of visuals are most appropriate for the occasion?
- What should I consider in the design?
- Do I give the audience enough time to read?
- Am I breaking eye contact?
- Have I anticipated problems?

## Reference

Weimer, M. (1993). *Improving your classroom teaching.* Newbury Park, CA: Sage.

# 10 | Handling Questions

*I'll answer some of your questions, the more difficult ones will be answered by my colleagues.*
   —Professor Roland Smith, Chairman, British Aerospace plc.

Tired? You should be. You have done a lot of work, and it is almost time for the show to begin. You have asked questions, planned your talk, and identified what, if any, visual reinforcement or clarification is required. By now you have also decided what you are going to wear. Before you go out there to face your public, you need to do more thinking about one other aspect of your talk. This chapter focuses on the time when you have ended your prepared speech and you become the receiver. It is question time. In fact, as we discussed in Chapter 7, there are some presentations that are all questions. In planning for your talk, seminar, workshop, or interview, you will have anticipated questions and/or objections and tried to understand the politics of the attendees as well, so you will have a good sense of people's perspectives. However, people will ask what they want to ask. The single most important recommendation is to maintain control of the event and of yourself; do not let an interview or speech slip away from you.

## Anticipate the Questions and Practice Some Responses

Knowing your subject as you do, you should have no problems with any question about the content. To repeat what was said earlier, a good way to prepare is to answer a few questions that a colleague or friend poses. Before you do that, however, it is time for more decisions. If you are giving a formal talk, you should ask yourself if you want questions. If so, when? Are they already built into the design, for example, 5 minutes at the end? Would you prefer to take some during the talk? If so, have you written yourself a note on your cards indicating that you need to tell the audience in the beginning that you will take questions during the talk? Will you field them yourself or will a moderator? Maybe you have decided that you will chat over coffee or that there will be no time for questions at all. Like so much else in presentation, you must make a decision about what works for the subject and for that audience.

## Watch the Time

Let's assume that you want to take questions and that rather than use an interactive approach, you want all the questions held until the end of your talk. How much time have you allotted for them? If it is 10 minutes, stick to that time. It is easy to lose control of the timing in this section of the presentation because one question or answer may lead to three or four more, so keep an eye on your watch.

## Pause Before Taking Questions

You have ended your talk with a solid closing. You have restated your objective or called the audience to action: "Therefore, I ask each of you to weigh the implications of . . ." Applause! "Thank you!" Pause. Change of pace. Change of tone, perhaps of location. Move to the right or left. "Are there any questions?" or "I would be delighted to take some questions." or "We have time for only three questions." In other words, you invite questions, and you do so with a smile on your face. This is not the time to look defensive. It is not the time to cross your arms on your chest and take two steps backward. It is the time to smile, to walk forward, and to look open, eager, and willing to take questions. How often have you seen a speaker look uncomfortable or defensive at this point in the presentation?

## Be Empathetic

Let's take a moment to reverse roles and think about how it feels to be in the audience. You have been there. Think about what most people do in an audience when it is question time. They spend time formulating the question and finding the right words, because asking a question in a room full of people is a minipresentation for the questioner. Therefore, people who ask questions need to be supported, so, as the speaker, show some empathy, please. Think of the times that you have sat in an audience wanting to ask a question but were reluctant to do so, fearful that you would sound stupid or that you would appear not to have been listening. Your mentor or dean could be in the room seeing you make a fool of yourself. With those scenarios in your mind, be warm and gracious when you take questions. No matter what you are asked, help the questioners retain their dignity. Be careful of demeaning or belittling the questioner with sarcasm. They will not articulate their gratitude to you, because they will not know that you are being empathetic, but they will appreciate your kindness and like you for it; that cannot hurt.

## Listen Carefully

As you are well aware, questions frequently have more to do with the questioner's need to be heard than they have to do with your talk. A little posturing may be involved. How often have you heard questioners end up telling of their own experiences or research findings or saying "I just wanted to say" and then going on at length and never asking a question? If that happens, be sure that you are listening. There may be a question after the preamble. Do not daydream or replay your talk. It is not over yet. Listen and use your skills—maintain eye contact and nod, if appropriate, to show that you are listening. Then be sure that you understand the question. You may have to say, "Do I understand you to mean _____?" Or you may want to repeat the question, bearing in mind that a question asked by someone in the front row may not be heard at the back of the room. Or you may want to paraphrase the question in words that are of your own choosing. The questioner says, "Aren't the implications catastrophic _____?" In response, you may want to select less emotive words: "While the implications have an impact, . . ."

## Answer the Entire Audience

When you answer the question, do not respond only to the questioner; address the room in an interview or answer the panel. You still have an obligation to everyone, and answering the question may give you the opportunity to reinforce a point or clarify a misunderstanding. Try not to end up in a conversation or dialogue with one person. In fact, if the question does provide an opportunity for you to reinforce a point that you've made, then for heaven's sake, thank the individual who asked it for raising the question, rather than looking angry or disgusted. Remember, you may want to repeat a question to ensure that everyone in the room has heard it.

## Keep Your Answers Brief

In addition, try not to make each of your answers too long. Just answer the question. If you have time for only three questions, you should not devote the entire time to one. Others will resent it. If you know someone's name, by all means use it.

## Maintain Your Own Dignity

If you get a hostile questioner, do not engage in combat. Do not be dragged into a fight. Keep your answers on a higher plane. Restate your points, but do not become rude or antagonistic. Usually, aggressive questioners will embarrass themselves, and the audience will admire your handling of the situation, if you are patient.

## Be Honest

Suppose you get a question and you genuinely do not know the answer to it. It does happen, but this is not the time for fiction. If what you are concerned with is maintaining or achieving credibility, then do not lie. There are no available data on presenters who have been struck dead by a thunderbolt for not knowing the answers to every question. You are not expected to be omniscient; however, you are more than capable of researching the answer. Being able to locate information is an important academic skill, so admit that you do not have the answer but that you can find it. Thank the questioner for asking it, promise to get the answer, and be sure that you do.

## Use Your Teaching Skills

If you have generated enthusiasm and animated discussion ensues, it is important to maintain control, as you would in class. Just as you might in a tutorial, rather than answer the questioner, person A, you may encourage person B to answer. Then person C might be asked to add to the discussion. What happens is that a discussion may develop among the members of the class, which may be wonderful, but unless you lead it like a conductor you will be left standing, looking on. The same is true with a presentation. In other words, if rather than answer a question yourself you want A to talk to B and C to add something, be sure that you, not A, B, or C, are determining when they have said enough. You invite D to speak, not watch while D chimes in. When you decide that the debate has gone on long enough, *you*, not they, end it.

Sometimes it is desirable to have the debate move away from you, because it allows members of the audience to get involved. You may get some useful feedback from what they are saying. Such interaction will indicate that you have created enough interest to have sparked some dialogue. Do not discourage it; just orchestrate it.

You have checked your watch. If time permits, ask if there are more questions. Wait briefly, then indicate that time is up. You make the decision to end the session. You may or may not want to restate your closing remarks. Either way, simply thank the audience, the moderator, or chair; smile; and go. You hold your head high. You look satisfied with the event. You do not roll your eyes, drop your shoulders, and exhale a great sigh. You are still on. You are being watched. You should sit down, shake hands, go back to your seat, or leave the room, walking tall and proud.

When handling questions, you should do the following:

- Anticipate the questions and practice some responses
- Watch the time
- Pause before taking questions
- Be empathetic
- Listen carefully
- Answer the entire audience
- Keep your answers brief
- Maintain your dignity
- Be honest
- Use your teaching skills

# 11 | Practicing and Planning

*Practice is everything.*

—Diogenes Laertius, Greek historian

Every aspect of presentation requires practice, and finding the time to do so is up to you. This chapter is about practicing. No coach can run the marathon or play the game for the athletes. Once you have the talk thought out and the points on your cards—even if the visuals are not completed yet—it is time for you to run through what you are going to say from beginning to end.

You practice your talk in part for timing, so put your watch on and start from the very beginning of the talk including your "Good morning" or "Good afternoon." Do not read it silently in your mind. Say it out loud, grope for the missing word, use your examples, tell your stories, and take pauses; as you do, think about where your visuals will be and start building in the pauses when you know that the audience will be looking at those visuals. If you recite the talk in your head, without the pause for the answer to the rhetorical question, for the laugh, or for the overhead, your timing will be inaccurate. All those little additions take time. As you are saying the words aloud, you also will be discovering what words should be empha-sized. You may want to actually underline them on the cards or draw parallel lines between them to indicate a pause after a key point.

You may also discover, as you hear what you are saying, that some data need to be added, clarified, or deleted. You may feel that you have too many arguments supporting your point, that one of your arguments is too weak to be included, or that something that recently occurred on campus might be a good example to fit in. You may discover that you need transitions to move you from one point to the next.

Practicing takes time, and you need to plan for it. By now you will have realized that presentation involves both a process and a product. Practicing is part of the process that refines the product, the speech itself. If you are using note cards, carry them with you, and, whenever you have a few minutes, take them out of your pocket or brief case and work through them; that way you increase your comfort level with your own notes.

## The Room

Now it is time for you to take a look at the room itself. This isn't always possible, but all you need is 10 or 15 minutes to reap enormous benefits. When you asked the question "where" in your preparation, you were probably given a description of the venue. Now it is time to walk around the room to see it and to get a feel for its idiosyncrasies. In effect, you are on reconnaissance. You enter with all your antenna, absorbing information. What are the acoustics like? Are there heavy drapes and carpets? Will your voice be absorbed by them? Speak out loud. Will your voice be heard in the back or will you need to use a microphone? If so, when will you have an opportunity to work with it?

What about the furniture? Are there tables and chairs? Are there only chairs there now, and will you need tables? Who provides them? When? What are the seats like? Straight-backed, hard seats or deeply cushioned ones, which are easier to relax or nod out in? How is the room arranged? Are the chairs in fixed positions, or can they be moved? Do you want the room in theater style or classroom style, or would you prefer a U-shape? The advantages of the latter are that there are fewer barriers coming between you and the audience and that the audience members can eyeball one another, not stare at the back of a neighbor's head.

What is at the front of the room for you? Is there a table, a lectern, or a dais? Are they movable? Will there be a head table? How big is it? Can you move around it with ease? Will it be covered by a cloth, or are your legs and feet clearly visible to the audience? How high will the table or lectern be? Can you be seen over it? Remember the pictures of Queen Elizabeth in Washington, D.C., a few years ago? Only her head and hat appeared over the lectern. Someone had forgotten to check the facilities before she started her speech.

What are the sight lines? In other words, when you are standing in the front of the room and if all seats are filled, can you be seen from every angle? Is there a pillar or a piece of equipment that blocks your view and that of the audience? Do you need to move chairs back or prevent people from sitting in certain seats? If you are using an overhead, at what angle are you blocked by it? If you are using a flip chart, where does it need to be placed for you to write comfortably and for the audience to see? Whether you are left handed or right handed will also determine where to position it. Are there enough pads for the flip chart? Are there pens or markers, pointers, erasers, or chalk? Where are the light switches? How dark is the room, with or without lights? Can people take notes? Are there wires or cables across the floor? Could you trip? Where are the outlets? Do you need additional extension cords?

Does the equipment work? Where are the power buttons? The volume control? The remote controls? Which button controls what? Is there someone other than yourself who could press some buttons? Is there room at the speaker's table for your acetates or a glass of water? Is where you are walking carpeted or will every footfall echo? Therefore, should you change your choice of shoes?

Are there windows? Is the room drafty? What is visible outside? Will people be walking by or is there heavy truck traffic? How public are you? Can the windows be opened or shut? How warm is the room when doors are closed? Warm enough for people to become sleepy? Will the air conditioning be on? If it has to be switched on or off during your talk, will the hum of the mechanism interfere with your being heard? How cold will it get? Are there any telephones? Will they ring? Can they be disconnected? Is there a PA system that will make the room sound like an airport or hospital? Can you control them? Are there doors that people in an outside corridor can inadvertently open? What's going on next door? Will it be noisy?

Details. Details. Details. Sound like a lot of work? It isn't really, perhaps 10 or 15 minutes worth. The answers to the above questions provide details that you are looking for when you go into the room. You are checking for possible problems, and you are checking to increase your own comfort level with it just the way a dog or cat does before snuggling down into his or her corner. Make the room your own and get comfortable with it.

## The Introductions

When you do your preparing, it is not all about the equipment, tables, and chairs. There are human elements as well. Will you be introducing yourself or will someone else be introducing you? If it is someone else, what do you want him or her to say or not say about you or your talk? As we mentioned earlier, sometimes the person introducing you can take a good line from your talk or misstate the intent of your talk, so chat with him or her in advance. Where will that person be sitting? Where will you be sitting in relation to that individual? What is the person's name? Can you pronounce it? Do you want that person to lead any posttalk questions or will you? Who will make concluding remarks?

If you are beginning to wonder if there are rules about all this, if one way is better than another, or whether one method is right and another is wrong, the answer is "No." It is right if you have thought through the implications of your decision and you are comfortable that it is the appropriate approach. Are you wondering why you should bother? Looking poised and at ease is more impressive than rushing into a room saying "Where do I speak from?" or "When do I start?" Your audience will not know when you have done your homework; they *will* know when you have *not*. There are enough spontaneous events that may occur during your talk, so why clutter your mind on the day of your presentation with extraneous details like locating switches that could have been found in advance in just a few minutes?

## Team Presentations

There is another aspect to your practicing and planning that needs to be addressed and that relates to your being a member of a team presentation. There is no difference in your planning except that you will have asked the questions together or shared the answers so that you all have a clear sense of your objectives. If you are working in a team, you will also need to divide the labor, to decide who is speaking on what aspect of your topic, and to compare notes on the data that each of you may be using and on the approach that each of you is taking.

A team presentation is not called that just because three or four people happen to be talking. It involves teamwork in its truest sense. The unique talents of the members of the football team are not brought together on the afternoon of a play-off game without an opportunity for the players to practice together in advance. When speaking, you must get used to one another's presentation styles—strengths, weaknesses, and how best to use or defuse them. Determine if, in terms of content, there is too much or too little overlap or none at all. Unless you talk among yourselves, one of you may make assumptions that the other person is handling some aspect that, in fact, is not being handled at all.

As a team, you also need to plan your own introductions. Will one of you be explaining who is going to say what; for example, "Frank will address the long-range plans, while I will be describing the current ones." Or will each of you introduce yourselves? How will you hand off the baton from one to the next? Just as you do as an individual, you also need to plan the question period. Which one of you will be taking which questions? Will one of you take all of the questions, or will you divide them up, depending on the focus? If you are hit with a tough one, what's the support system?

You will also need to decide about the seating arrangements. Will each of you walk up from the audience or table? During the questions, will you all be standing? How will you refer to each other: "my colleague, Jim" or "Jim"? When you pass the baton, will you be "handing over" to Donna, or will you have a sentence that reintroduces Donna's section; for example, "Donna will now discuss the reasons for _____ " or "Donna is better able to _____ ."

Know that in a team presentation everyone is being watched, not just the speaker at the moment. It is remarkable how often in team presentations the members look as though they have no use for one another. They look stone faced. They do not listen when the other members speak. You should create the impression that you like one another, that you work together, and that you care about one another. You do that by looking interested in what the other person is saying and by listening and reacting to your colleagues' words. If there is a joke, smile at it. If one of you makes a mistake, the other one should be ready to pick up.

In other words, practicing is about controlling your environment to free you from unnecessary additional anxieties. Therefore, you need to build in the time to do the following:

- Run through your own talk to refine and time it.
- Examine the venue, the layout, and the equipment.
- Plan the introductions.
- Plan and practice together if you are part of a team.

# 12 | Handling Your Nerves

*You have no reason to fear the wind if your hay-bales are tied
down.*

—Irish proverb

*Considering how dangerous everything is, nothing is really very
frightening.*

—Gertrude Stein

Now that the time for your presentation is nearing, you are
probably experiencing some self-doubts. This chapter is devoted to your worries and offers some thoughts about handling them. First of all, understand that you will always be
nervous before you talk. Stage fright is normal. A little ad-
renaline energizes the team, the athlete, the dancer, or the
speaker. There is no reason to be ashamed or embarrassed. For
most people, nervousness does not last long into the performance; it fades quickly. However, to better understand your
own "fight-or-flight" response, it is helpful to become more
self-aware. In other words, learn to recognize your own reactions when you are under stress and then accept or compensate
for them. By doing so you can also diminish them.

## Prepare

The best cure for nerves, if there is one, is to do your homework so that you are prepared. The better you know the

material, the audience, and the venue, the less anxious you will be. Running through your material in the room in advance also increases your comfort level. In addition, rather than berating yourself for feeling nervous, remember that everyone gets nervous, not just you. We are all affected by the jitters in different ways. If you ask, you will discover that some people find that their palms or underarms are drenched with sweat. Some begin to feel their hearts pounding in their chests. Do you remember the expression, "My heart was in my mouth"? Others have a "hollow feeling" in the pit of their stomach. Still others feel heat around their faces, and their necks are flushed. Still others feel the strength ebb from their legs, and their hands tremble. In others, throats go dry. Some go to the bathroom more often. Do you recognize any of these symptoms? If you do, you have probably also noticed that the sensations ease as you gain control of your body and of the situation early in your talk.

Please note that this chapter is called "Handling Your Nerves," not "Curing Your Nerves." It is important to accept the fact that some nervousness is normal; however, there are some techniques that may ease the symptoms or at least help you compensate for them.

## Consider What to Drink

For example, many people find that having a cup of tea or coffee before giving a talk helps them to focus their minds. It may. It may also heighten your anxiety. Eliminating caffeine is one of the first suggestions for people who fear flying. Coffee is also a diuretic, so you may find yourself going off to the bathroom one more time. Consider, therefore, forgoing that last cup or two. That is particularly true if you have a sensitive stomach. Instead, you might have some room-temperature water near where you are speaking. It is even more important if you know that your mouth tends to go dry. By the way, taking a sip is also a great excuse for a well-timed pause.

## Know the Route to the Dais

If your legs do not quite feel as if they will hold you up, be sure that you know the route that takes you from where you are sitting to where you are speaking. Practice walking the path, especially if there are any steps that you might have to climb or descend. If there is a banister, hold on to it.

## Avoid Magnifying Your Hands

It is natural to worry that the audience will notice your trembling hands. Do not be concerned. They won't. When your hands are at their worst, the audience is looking at the warm expression on your face and are focused on your opening remarks. However, if you do not want to draw attention to your shaking hands, be sure that you have your first acetate already placed on the overhead projector before turning on the switch. You do not want the shadow of a trembling hand magnified and filling the screen for all of the audience to see.

## Have Notes

Suppose your fear, though, is that you are going to panic and forget everything you had planned to say. Although we talked in Chapter 8 about using notes, it is important to mention their use here. The day that I went blank in front of the camera, I had *no* notes. I learned a lesson. Use notes. Consider writing down your opening sentences word for word on one card. If you have worked yourself into a state of panic as I had, the precise words will be written down for you to know why you are speaking and what the subject is. As you ease into the next few sentences, the anxiety will be fading.

## Take the Focus Off Yourself

Remember that it is when you first begin your talk that you are most anxious; therefore, you may want to take the attention off yourself by creating a diversion, that is, by designing an opening that moves the focus from you to something else. For example, you might ask the audience members to talk briefly to one another about something you have planned, have a visual projected on the screen, or have a question preflipped. By doing that you will involve the audience in the activity or have them looking at something other than you and your hands.

## "Think Happy Thoughts"

There are other techniques as well. It is important to remember that you are knocking the stuffing out of yourself with your self-doubts. First of all, remember the answer to "why me?": Because we know you can do it; because you know more about the topic than anyone else, and so on. To ease stress of any kind, find the time to make a list of your accomplishments and keep it handy. Refer to it in advance of any stressful situation. You may say that you do not have any accomplishments, but you do, realistic ones. Getting your last degree, writing an article, designing a course, mentoring an undergraduate, winning a particular tournament, or finishing a certain project are accomplishments. We are not looking for lists that start off with "winning the Nobel Prize." Just list things that you are proud of and that made you feel good. Peter Pan enabled the Darling children to fly by encouraging them to be positive. You can soar as well.

In advance of the speech, look at the list to remind yourself that you are a winner. What you are doing is replacing negative thoughts with positive ones.

## Visualize a Relaxing Scene

In addition, consider taking a moment or two to go off on your own to calm yourself down. Close your eyes and visualize a tranquil place or moment that you have experienced. It may be a deserted beach, a quiet forest scene, or the water of a lake gently lapping against the shore. By closing your eyes and concentrating on that peaceful scene, you will relax.

## Breathe Deeply

In addition, take some good deep breaths and release them slowly. That is a particularly good idea when you are just about to speak. It is also one of the reasons why you need to stand tall with your chest up. Good posture enhances your ability to fill your lungs. Not only does it improve your voice, but those deep breaths, rather than shallow ones, can also calm you. Do not begin to talk until you are ready and you have taken a good deep breath.

## Take a Walk

You should treat nerves the way you do stress of any kind; therefore, the recommendations are the same, including finding a few minutes to stretch your legs. Rather than pace in your office, take a brisk 10-minute walk.

## Analyze the Fears

Suppose you are still making yourself crazy. Take one of your self-doubts and follow it to its natural conclusion. In other words, if you hear, "I will be desperate!" in your own mind, focus on it and start analyzing it by asking yourself questions. Well, now what will be terrible? Why? Then what will happen to me if it happens? And then what? Force your mind to address the thought and take it to its logical conclusion. If you do, you will see that the outcomes are unrealistic. You are not going to die, be ostracized, exiled, imprisoned, or lose your job. In essence, try to ease the stress with positive physical and mental activity.

Being nervous is normal, and, as you all know, nervousness fades quickly. However, you may ease the anxiety if you do the following:

- Prepare
- Consider what to drink
- Know the route to the dais
- Avoid magnifying your hands
- Have notes
- Take the focus off yourself
- "Think happy thoughts"
- Visualize a relaxing scene
- Breathe deeply
- Take a walk
- Analyze the fears

# 13 | It's Show Time!

*The ability to speak is a short cut to distinction. It puts a man in the limelight, raises him head and shoulders above the crowd, and the man who can speak acceptably is usually given credit for an ability out of all proportion to what he really possesses.*
    —Lowell Thomas, American journalist

You have done your planning. You have asked your questions, you have written the material, and you are looking good: Shoes shined, hair trimmed, notes in hand, visuals in order, and thoughts positive. It's show time! But you are not quite finished yet. There is more to do. Remember the decisions you make are before, during, and after.

## Listen to Other Speakers

Suppose your talk is part of a lengthier discussion or that you are one of a series of speakers. Then, on the day, you should be listening to what the others are speaking about before it is your turn. You do that to be able to modify your own speech based on what you have heard someone else say. For example, you may find that you disagree with another speaker, agree with or like a particular phrase that was used, or realize that one of the other speakers has said something you had planned to say. So use it: "As Adam said earlier, _____" or "As Harry said, I must disagree that _____" or "There is no need for me to explain what Marcia stated so clearly but

_____ ." Besides looking professional, you are role modeling good listening skills for your audience.

## Incorporate Current Events

In addition, on the day of your talk be aware of any noteworthy events that are currently in the news. There may be a major tournament, a sports trade, a literary award, a national election, or 100-mile-per-hour winds. You might be able to incorporate one of the events into your talk as an analogy or example. Doing that may bring your message home once again or bring it to life.

## Be Open About Mistakes

By now, you have done all the planning and anticipating that you can do. It is now time to think on your feet, to handle whatever happens spontaneously as it occurs, and to make instant decisions. Some you may anticipate, others you will not. Let's suppose you have been introduced. You have begun—the audience is with you, all is well, but you make a mistake. You lose your train of thought, you misuse a word, or you drop one of your note cards. Do not try to hide it. It happened. The audience may welcome the fact that you are being human and as humans, we are fallible, so make the mistake and make it big. Smile, laugh, apologize. Collect your thoughts, find the right word, or bend down and pick up the card. If you are quick-witted, you may be able to incorporate some aspect of the error into your talk. Then let it go. It has happened, and it is over, like a mishit in tennis. You mishit the ball. Now there is another point to play. If you dwell on the error, there may be another mishit. What does every sports announcer say? "_____ has lost concentration." Regain yours.

## Handle Disruptions With Charm

Now suppose you are well into your talk, and two people enter the room late. Make an assessment. If you see members of the audience turning to look, comment, or acknowledge the latecomers, remember that at that moment you are not being listened to. So stop. Look pleasant. No point looking annoyed. Why make the newcomers feel more uncomfortable than they probably already are? Diffuse their discomfort with a smile. You are looking for friends, not enemies. Once they are settled, continue. Depending on how many or who, you may want to make a one-or-two sentence recap or indicate that "we were making the point that _____ ."

## Gauge Your Audience's Reactions

Well, you have had your error and your interruption. Do you think that now you can go on some sort of automatic pilot? No! Remember what was said about eye contact: Look and see what is happening. You need to be using the antenna again, this time to take in the smiles, the frowns, the glazed eyes, the doodling or note-taking, and the side conversations. If you sense that the audience is beginning to fatigue or to lose interest, you know that you need to make a change.

## Respond to What You Are Seeing

Based on your knowledge of your own repertoire of talents, make a change and decide to do something different from what you are doing. This shift of tempo is like a symphony, with each movement written in a different tempo. Maybe it is time to walk or to move more quickly. Maybe you have not played with your voice at all, so it is time to change the volume, take it down to a whisper, or raise it. Do you think what you have been saying is too complicated or abstract? When did you notice that the audience started to fade? Is it time for a quick recap or for an example or anecdote? Should you have a window opened? Should you take a break? Should you eliminate an entire upcoming section that you had planned to discuss? Should you take questions? Based on what is happening at the moment, you need to make a decision, to react, or to do something different. What you choose to do is entirely up to you. By watching and gauging reactions and by making changes you will keep the presentation lively and energized. With your audience uppermost in your thoughts, you will be reacting to them and keeping them with you.

## Think About What Worked and What You Would Have Done Differently

You have done it! Bask in the applause and pat yourself on the back. Sure, be relieved, but enjoy and be proud of what you have done. The audience will let you know that you did a good job. They will not know all the work that you put into preparation, but the effort you have spent has brought success. Like any professional, you made it look easy. When the presentation is over, you will be tired, possibly drained. Maintaining a high degree of concentration during a talk is fatiguing. While the event is still reasonably fresh in your mind, replay your own mental tape of the proceedings. Do not be hypercritical or start to nitpick—oh, I put my hand in my pocket four times, I said "um" too often, I looked at one side of the room too much. OK, you did. Pat yourself on the back for the things you did right, and know that in time old habits will give way to new and better ones. So look at the big picture. Did the opening work? Were your arguments clear? Did the questions suggest that the audience understood your message?

## Ask for Feedback

Find out what people liked and what worked. Get some feedback from others; do not just rely on your own self-assessment. Listen to what people recall. Was it what you wanted them to remember? All of this data is added to your growing wealth of information, ideas, techniques, or approaches that seem to work for you or that may not. Learn from what you did to apply it to the next talk. Experiment.

## Develop a Critical Eye

In addition to your own self-assessment and feedback from friends, colleagues, and attendees, start observing other people. Look at people. Watch other speakers. Look at the way accomplished speakers dress. Look at their hair, the color combinations, the fit of their clothes, and their choice of jewelry. Look at TV, watch the news, and go to the movies. Every time you do, every time you sit in a meeting, watch the speaker, watch the movement, and observe the speech pattern, the facial expressions, the use of the hands, how mistakes are handled, how questions are handled, what visuals were used, and what new technology is used. Ask yourself if it worked. Watch and listen to the audience. Develop a critical eye about what appears to be effective and what is not. Start saving stories or anecdotes for further reference. Most of all, look for excuses to speak again. Every time you stand up and speak you will be developing your skills with your students as well. At the end of the day, presenting should be seen as an opportunity for you as an individual to shine and, therefore, for your department, college, or university to shine as well.

On the day of your talk, you should do the following:

- Listen to other speakers
- Incorporate current events

- Be open about mistakes
- Handle disruptions with charm
- Gauge your audience's reactions
- Respond to what you are seeing
- Think about what worked and what you would have done differently
- Ask for feedback
- Develop a critical eye

Being able to give a good presentation is an important skill in today's competitive environment. A person who can prepare and deliver an effective talk is an asset to any organization and welcome at any conference. Someone who can explain, motivate, persuade, tell, encourage, and entertain others is invaluable, because such people can create new avenues for research, encourage students and colleagues, explain ideas clearly, articulate problems, present alternatives, and justify decisions. When they do, people listen.

You can be such a person. Understand the principles and practice the skills. You may still say to yourself, "I'll be OK," "I'll be fine," or "It will be over soon." However, say it no longer as a passive, dependent individual filled with anxiety, but rather from a position of knowledge and strength. The emphasis changes as well, because now, you *will* be OK, you *will* be fine, and, yes, it *will* be over soon. But undoubtedly there will be another day, another talk, or another opportunity, because people will listen to you.

# Additional Resources

Argyle, M. (1988). *The psychology of interpersonal behaviour* (4th ed.). London: Pelican.

*The articulate executive: Orchestrating effective communication* with a preface by Fernando Bartolome. (1993). Boston: Harvard Business School Press.

Brownell, J. (1986). *Building active listening skills.* Englewood Cliffs, NJ: Prentice Hall.

Davis, K., & Newstrom, J. (1989). *Human behavior at work.* New York: McGraw-Hill.

Decker, B. (1988). *The art of communicating.* Los Altos, CA: Crisp.

Farb, P. (1974). *Word play.* New York: Pocket Books.

Fast, J. (1970). *Body language.* New York: Pocket Books.

Fox, J., & Levin, J. (1993). *How to work with the media.* Newbury Park, CA: Sage.

Goffman, E. (1959). *The presentation of self in everyday life.* Garden City, NY: Doubleday.

Goffman, E. (1971). *Relations in public.* New York: Basic Books.

Goodall, H., & Waagen, C. (1986). *Persuasive presentation.* New York: Harper & Row.

Hall, E. (1959). *The silent language.* Garden City, NY: Doubleday.

Hall, E. (1966). *The hidden dimension.* Garden City, NY: Doubleday.

Janner, G. (1989). *Janner on presentation.* London: Business Books.

Peel, M. (1990). *Improving your communication skills.* London: Kogan Page.

Peoples, D. A. (1988). *Presentations plus.* New York: John Wiley.

Richards, J. (1988). *How to give a successful presentation.* Norwell, MA: Graham & Trotman.

Stanton, N. (1990). *Communication.* London: Macmillan.

Steil, L., Summerfield, J., & de Mare, G. (1983). *Listening: It can change your life.* New York: John Wiley.

Thompson, J. (1973). *Beyond words.* New York: Scholastic.

Weimer, M. (1993). *Improving your classroom teaching.* Newbury Park, CA: Sage.

Wells, G. (1986). *How to communicate.* London: McGraw-Hill.

# About the Author

Elizabeth P. Tierney is a trainer, speaker, and consultant in both academia and industry. She has lectured in business ethics and organizational behavior at University College, Dublin, Ireland, as well as consulting in the Graduate School, and has worked with junior and senior managers and academics in Ireland, Northern Ireland, Hungary, and the United States. She holds a doctorate in educational administration from Fordham University. In the United States, she worked in various administrative positions. Her interests and expertise include such areas of management development as communication, trainer training, and business ethics. The author of *Selling Yourself: A Practical Guide to Job Hunting*, she is currently working on other books in business ethics and management. She now divides her time between the United States and Ireland.